Zero to One Million Followers with Social Media Marketing Viral Secrets

Learn How Top Entrepreneurs Are Crushing It with YouTube, Facebook, Instagram, And Influencer Network Branding Ads

Gary Jake

Legal Notice:

This book is copyright protected. This book is only for personal use. You cannot amend, distribute, sell, use, quote or paraphrase any part, or the content within this book, without the consent of the author or publisher.

Disclaimer Notice:

Please note the information contained within this document is for educational and entertainment purposes only. All effort has been executed to present accurate, up to date, and reliable, complete information. No warranties of any kind are declared or implied. Readers acknowledge that the author is not engaging in the rendering of legal, financial, medical or professional advice. The content within this book has been derived from various sources. Please consult a licensed professional before attempting any techniques outlined in this book.

By reading this document, the reader agrees that under no circumstances is the author responsible for any losses, direct or indirect, which are incurred as a result of the use of information contained within this document, including, but not limited to, — errors, omissions, or inaccuracies.

Contents

2 IN 1 VALUE

ZERO
TO ONE

MILLION FOLLOWERS

WITH SOCIAL MEDIA MARKETING VIRAL SECRETS

LEARN HOW TOP ENTREPRENEURS ARE CRUSHING
IT WITH **YOUTUBE, FACEBOOK, INSTAGRAM,** AND
INFLUENCER NETWORK BRANDING ADS

GARY JAKE

From Zero to One Million Followers

Become an Influencer with Social Media Viral Growth Strategies on YouTube, Twitter, Facebook, Instagram, and the Secrets to Make Your Personal Brand KNOWN

Chapter 1:
The Future of Branding is Going Digital

A new era of branding has emerged. The focus has shifted from product and corporate branding to personal branding. Personal branding is taking the leading role compared to a few years ago. Companies are also keying into the trend of personal branding and obtaining its benefits.

Why Personal Branding?

Is there any difference between corporate branding and personal branding? Personal branding is quite different from corporate branding. Personal branding has to do with the perception of an individual. It's a process whereby individuals attach value to themselves by creating a positive image of their personality. Corporate branding, on the other hand, concerns how a company or organization packages itself or its products to boost sales. The only similarity between corporate and personal branding is that they both involve striving to create a positive and professional image. People are more likely to relate to a personal brand more than a corporate one. Therefore, most companies and organizations love to associate with a public figure who has a strong personal brand. They have a unique, human touch to them that most corporate brands lack. They have experiences and emotions that the average person can relate to and wants to associate with. Therefore, it is advisable to have a personal brand first if you want to create your own company or business. It's not enough to create a personal brand; you must keep your brand aligned with the interests of your target audience. Every day, new trends are being churned out, and it would be in your interests to incorporate a few of these trends into your personal brand to make it come alive. One such trend is podcasts. Podcasts have existed for years now, but only a few brands have utilized their value to personal branding. Podcasts help your brand to reach a wider audience and equally create familiarity between your brand and your audience.

Previously, the scope of branding was limited to business cards, or a few newspapers and that was it. However, in this age, branding has been moved and is still moving towards a digital dimension.

How Is Branding Going Digital?

When most companies or organizations want to develop their brand, they rarely place ads in newspapers or magazines. Even if they do, it is merely a secondary means of creating awareness for their brand to the minor percentage of people who do not have any social media platforms. Their primary tool for creating awareness is through social media platforms, digital billboards, and TV commercials.

Technology is advancing, and as such, they must change their means of giving vital information and content. The fact that branding is going digital implies that as a brand owner and developer, you need to strategize and develop new ways to make your brand stand out from the crowds of brands that pop up on people's screens daily. If you stay active on social media for just one hour, you are bound to notice about fifteen different brands, both personal and corporate, pop up on your screen. The status quo is no longer enough for brand growth and development. For your brand to thrive and win the loyalty and interest of your audience, you need to be unique, original and authentic. Study a common trend among similar brands in your industry and produce your own variation of it.

Social media platforms have more influence on your brand than traditional newspaper ads. Therefore, we have so many social media influencers out there hitting it big. Social media platforms have a way of bringing your brand to life and putting it out there for the world to see. The average modern person is active on at least two social media platforms. When your brand is projected on these platforms, you get an increased engagement and interaction with potential customers. To fully utilize the power of social media for your brand, you need an understanding of the intricacies of social media platforms. First, define your target audience. Are you aiming to reach entrepreneurs, college students, or people whose interests are aligned with yours?

Define who your target audience is and employ the various social media tools within your reach to get to them.

If you want your brand to thrive on social media, you must follow certain guidelines. You need to have a deep knowledge and insight into what social media users want to see and hear. Personal branding isn't just about creating a brand and displaying it on social media for the world to see. You need to align your brand with the interests of your target audience and design it in a way that would make your brand seem new and fresh. Discover the tactics which social media influencers apply to keep people interested and engaged. How do they create and maintain their large following? How do they keep their audience interested and their brand popular? As you go further into this book, you will discover these secrets.

Your brand needs to be interesting and relevant. Although social media is beneficial to your brand, it is equally demanding and unforgiving. Social media has no place for mediocrity. If you don't churn out interesting, lively content regularly, your audience will get bored and move on. The major key to keeping your audience interested in whatever you have to say is by having and maintaining a standard. If your brand is known for always presenting relevant information and content, people will troop to your page to learn more. Posting boring or incorrect content will put a mark of unreliability on your brand.

Note that you do not have to be on every social media platform to develop your brand. All you must do is to pick the top platforms for your brand. The first thing to consider when selecting social media platforms for brand development is user demographics. How many people use this app? What is the age range of frequent users? What gender makes up the highest percentage of users? The user demographic must be in line with your target audience.

Another factor to consider is the value and content of your personal brand. If your brand is one that revolves around visual display, then the top social media platform you should consider is Instagram. If your brand revolves around content creation, then Facebook or YouTube might be your best bet.

Why Is Social Media So Important for Your Personal Brand?

Social media creates recognition for your brand. Constant content creation on social media platforms would link your brand with your target audience and create easy brand recognition. Thus, your brand is put on the map.

Without social media, it would be a herculean task to reach your target audience, because most people these days would rather be online than read a newspaper.

It is the fastest and most effective avenue for you to market yourself and what you do. Social media platforms carry news and topics faster than any other channel. For example, you could open your Twitter app one day and see a trending hashtag with over a million tweets relating to it. You need to utilize this power of social media for your brand.

Social media platforms create an opportunity for your brand's voice to be heard. Most people develop their personal brands to make an impact on society and to add value. For example, let's assume your personal brand revolves around content creation. You can display your content creating skills and make an impact through social media. Imagine your talent is an object on the ground level, and there's a crowd of people standing around. This crowd would not be motivated to look down to see the object. Now, if the object is raised on a platform high enough for people to see, a level of interest and curiosity would be aroused in the crowd, and they would be eager to know what the object is. That is exactly how social media works.

Social media is also an avenue for learning. It gives you the opportunity to gain more knowledge and insight about personal branding. With social media, you can study similar brands within your industry and learn from them. Experts on branding share vital information and tips on different platforms daily. You can apply those tips to improve your personal brand.

In addition to the above benefits, social media equally enables you to build a relationship between your brand and your target audience. It should be noted that building relationships with both your audience and other brands is key to having a strong personal brand. Constant engagement and interaction with your audience would create a relationship and bring about brand loyalty.

The Dos and Don'ts of Social Media

Thousands of brands have been developed on social media platforms. However, some have equally failed because they did not adhere to the basic dos and don'ts of social media.

Don't jump onto every trending topic on social media. Your brand needs to maintain a certain level of dignity and class. Hopping onto every topic would make your brand seem unprofessional and tacky. It might be tempting or appealing to make a comment on certain trending topics, but you should know where to draw the line. How relevant is the topic to your brand? Topics that are irrelevant or cannot be linked to your brand should be avoided at all costs. Unless your personal brand is a gossip blog, you do not necessarily have to put up content relating to gossip or anything of the sort. Avoid unnecessary controversy. One of the biggest myths about branding is that controversy sells. This is a false assumption. Controversy could hurt or taint your brand. Some brands have been involved in one controversy or the other and eventually recovered from it. Some brands have also been sold through controversy. However, your case might be different. Social media controversy has the power to either make or mar your brand. Your personal brand might never recover if you decide to make it controversial. Know what works for your brand and stick to it.

Move with the times and trends. Social media keeps adapting and changing each day. If you don't move with the times, your brand will become stagnant and eventually become out of date. The fastest way to lose brand relevance is by staying stagnant. For example, one of the ways to prevent the stagnation of your brand is to use up-to-date tools on social media platforms. Before the innovation of sponsored adverts on social media, people merely marketed their brands using hashtags and optimized keywords. However, since sponsored adverts and promotions became a thing on social media, brands have utilized that tool to gain a wider reach. Now imagine a brand that still depends solely on hashtags without employing new social media tools. The brand's growth rate would be slower in comparison with other modern brands.

Do not mix with the wrong crowd on social media. Tread with caution. Your audience watches your interaction and the relationships you build. The brands and people you associate with on social media could change your audience's perception of you and your personal brand. This change could either be positive or negative. Meticulously pick out the brands you want to build an online relationship with and weigh the consequences of such a relationship. It is apparent that brands with negative reputations could damage your brand. On the other hand, partnering with highly reputable brands will boost your personal brand.

Try as much as possible to avoid cluttering your timeline. Creating content for your social media handles is crucial. But it shouldn't be overdone. Making a hundred Facebook posts or tweets a day is quite unhealthy for your brand. Initially, your audience will be glad to see frequent posts from your brand. If you continue posting and reposting for hours, they'll get bored and scroll past. Their interest will soon wane if you post excessively.

Have a relationship with your audience. Relate with your audience like you relate with other people in your everyday life. Think of them as your friends and relate with them the same way. This makes you not only relatable, but it also gives your account a friendly outlook and can increase your followers. One of the ways you can engage your audience is by asking open ended questions on your page. You can ask questions relating to the season. For example, during the valentine season, you can ask them to talk about their first valentine experience in the comment section. When you ask questions like this, try to reply some if not all the comments. A reply as short as an emoji can make them feel loved and relevant. Even if you do not reply all the comments, your followers will interact with each other and might even invite their friends to join in the conversation. If on twitter you can encourage your followers to include a hashtag created by you in their comments, this increases the chance of your hashtag trending and can put your account on the spotlight.

As a personal brand, your social media presence needs to have a professional outlook. Remember you are creating a brand and not just another social media account. Your account should show how intentional you are.

How Do You Look More Professional on Your Social Media Platforms?

The first step to having a professional social media presence is to ensure that all your social media handles look professional. Start by picking out a very professional username. Your username could be your full personal name or the name you've chosen for your brand. Tacky nicknames should be avoided at all costs. Also, a professional looking picture of you should be used as your profile picture and cover photo. Pictures of you in compromising positions should be disposed of. Your profile pictures should be of high quality. Blurry or grainy pictures would make your profile seem substandard. Avoid using a group picture on your profile picture. You are trying to build a brand and people might get confused when they see two or more people instead of just you on your profile picture. Let your face be associated with your brand. If at all, you want to put others on your profile picture, do not let it be there for so long. Another thing that can make your handles look professional is your "bio." This is the first message people see when they visit your page. Make it short, concise, catchy and very interesting to read.

Another step to having a professional social media presence is to audit your past completely. The internet is a veritable store of information. Your history can be dug up with just a few clicks. A lot of notable personalities have lost their reputations or job opportunities simply because an old social media post or article was discovered. Clear out any incriminating articles or pictures of you on the web. Delete unnecessary tags and posts. If you had previously made any press statements that would be contradictory to what your personal brand currently represents, make attempts to remove them from the web.

Endeavor to use relevant hashtags. Social media algorithms work in such a way that posts are found by using optimized hashtags and keywords. Using irrelevant hashtags would make your posts cluttered. Personal brand experts know the right keywords to use, depending on the content of each post. In subsequent chapters, you will be taught how to utilize relevant hashtags and understand how social media algorithms work. Also, ensure that your social media posts are free of grammatical errors. Proofread your posts before sending them out. You don't want to appear unprofessional or ignorant.

Edit your privacy settings on all social media platforms. As a personal brand, you have no business with a private profile. When your potential audience or customers stumble upon your page or profile, your privacy settings might put them off. Make your profile public. Similarly, your profile bio should be updated regularly. Don't maintain the same bio for years. It will get old and boring. Update your bio but maintain a consistent message at the same time.

One mark of a professional personal brand is activeness. Are you active on all your social media platforms? Try as much as possible to be active to keep your audience entertained. If you have any opinions on an issue or topic, present those opinions appropriately and professionally.

The need for professionalism on social media cannot be overstated because you represent your personal brand and vice-versa.

Chapter 2:
What Your Personal Brand Must Accomplish

When you ask people about the factor that makes an individual powerful, most people's reply would be, "success." However, most people don't know what makes a personal brand powerful. For a brand to be considered powerful, it needs to possess certain qualities.

Strong personal brands are credible. There must be a level of credibility for your audience to trust your brand. How do you build brand credibility? First, you must create an effective strategy for marketing your brand. Ensure that your personal brand has a wide outreach and following. Brands with a large audience are often considered more credible than others.

Also, to create full credibility, you should make use of a third-party credibility system. When your brand is referred to and talked about by other influencers and developers, a mark of credibility is sealed on it. Interact with other brand owners and ask them to refer your brand to others. People are more likely to believe a brand's credibility when they hear about it from a third party. Let's assume that a new drink company launched a new product. You would be reluctant to try out any of their drinks unless someone you hold in high esteem vouches for them. This is how third-party credibility is built through referrals from both large scale and small-scale influencers.

A strong personal brand should equally be consistent in its content. For example, if your personal brand creates content based on graphic design or style, do not suddenly switch to a completely different theme. Don't suddenly drop off the radar and expect your brand to keep on thriving. Once your brand dropped off the radar, your audience would move to the next available brand. Consistency makes your personal brand more reliable and dependable and creates brand loyalty and trust. Most brand owners underestimate the power of brand consistency. If your brand is inconsistent in its content and marketing, it will lack definition, and you'll begin to lose your audience.

For your personal brand to be strong, it must be visible. Personal brands are like random products in a supermarket that has no assistants apart from a cashier. The more visible products get purchased by people within a short period of time and are often restocked faster. On the other hand, the products hidden in dark corners don't get purchased. It takes a meticulous customer to notice them. Often, they'd gather dust in those corners until someone finally notices them and purchases them or places them on a more visible shelf. Your brand needs to be bold and visible in order to reach your target audience. Use the social media tools within your disposal. Utilize SEO keywords. If your personal brand isn't visible, it won't grow.

One quality that every strong personal brand possesses is engagement. Your personal brand should create engagement with your audience. It should not be a one-way measure. Create an opportunity for your audience to engage and interact with you. In college, everyone's favorite professor isn't the one who stands in front of the class to read out his lecture notes. The favorite professor is the one who engages and interacts with his students, asking questions and giving them room to explain and air their opinions. Your personal brand should adequately engage your audience. This will encourage the audience to keep coming back for more.

Strong personal brands are also professional. Set a standard for your brand and maintain that standard.

Another factor that makes a personal brand powerful is authenticity. Your brand needs to be authentic and original. You can make your personal brand authentic by letting your personality shine through. People need to know that you are real, and they can relate to you and your content. Do not create an unrealistic image or standard of yourself as it would immediately put your audience off.

Your Brand Personality
Your brand personality is the perception your audience and consumers have about your brand. This is what personal branding and branding revolves around. You need to create the perfect brand personality to draw your target audience closer to you.

The first step to creating the perfect brand personality is to strategize. Research on different brand personalities. You can't create a positive brand personality if you don't have an in-depth knowledge of how it works. Define what you want for your brand and prepare to take the necessary steps to achieve your desired result.

The next step to take towards creating a brand personality is to determine the goal of your brand. What do you want your personal brand to revolve around? The goal of your personal brand determines what your brand personality would be like. Different brands require different personalities. Some personal brands have aggressive personalities, others have empathic personalities and so on. Once you have outlined the goal of your brand, you can go on to create a brand personality.

Before creating your brand personality, ask yourself some questions. You need to harness your positive personality traits and bring them to light. Define your personality first.

- Are you aggressive?

- Can you multitask?

- Are you introverted?

- What is your area of expertise?

The point here is to quiz yourself to understand your personality and decide which traits of yours should be reflected in your personal brand.

To create a good brand personality, you need to study other competing brands. Study the different brand personalities of similar brands within your industry. The essence of this is to understand their brand personalities and how it works for them and work on creating something unique. Don't try to imitate their brand personalities as there can be only one original. Create a personality that will stand out from the others.

After following the steps above, the final step is to scrutinize and analyze your personal brand. Ensure that it corresponds with your personality. If there are hitches, you may need to amend those. Ascertain that there are no contradictions whatsoever in your personal brand. Your personal brand should be flexible and amenable to slight changes.

The Basic Rules of Personal Branding

Personal branding has a set of rules that will guide you to success. The first rule of personal branding is:

Don't stop creating content. Your brand should always have relevant, veritable content to share. This does not mean that you should choke your audience with every piece of information you come across. What it means is that you should set a daily target for making posts on your social media handles or website. Determine the appropriate number of posts that should be made daily and work with that target. Your content should keep your audience hooked and eager for more. Make efforts to ensure that you don't sound boring or repetitive like a cracked record.

In the same vein, much thought should be put into your content. Your personal brand can be damaged by just one simple post. Before you post, carefully gauge what you've written so far. Don't just post the first thing that comes to your mind. Scrutinize your posts and ensure that it is relevant to your brand. Check for any sentence or element that may be offensive to a group of people. Scan the post to ensure that it is appropriate, correct and well organized. Also, scan your posts for grammatical errors that would make your brand look un-professional.

Don't come across as desperate. Although the main aim of branding is to sell yourself and what you do, you do not want to make your brand look desperate. Some personal brands try so hard to sell themselves and gain relevance, that they end up going extreme. Avoid disturbing or confusing your audience. Don't try too hard to seek attention and relevance. In this age of social media, people can smell desperation from ten miles away. Set a high standard for your brand and stick to it. Your personal brand would command no respect if your audience feels that you are desperate.

Personal branding is about creating the best possible image of yourself and selling it. As such, your strengths and not your weaknesses should be highlighted. People want to know that they are dealing with a reliable brand. For example, when a person wants to buy a smartphone, he doesn't go for a phone whose weaknesses outnumber its strengths. It would be a liability. Instead, he buys the opposite. Similarly, your audience would not want to associate with your brand if your weaknesses are more pronounced than your strengths. Thus, you should portray yourself and your brand in a positive light.

Don't sell a false image of yourself. Since, it is advisable to create a positive perception of yourself, do not falsify the facts to seem extraordinary. A personal branding expert should know how to sell himself or herself without resorting to falsehood. When you create a fake image of your personal brand, contradiction is bound to happen eventually. Once your personal brand contradicts itself, it loses its reputation and audience. It's just like buying a box of cereal, and when you finally pour out the content of the box into a bowl, all you see is broken glass. You would not buy that cereal brand again, and you would make sure that your friends didn't, either. That is exactly what happens when you project a false perception of yourself in personal branding.

Do not be afraid to take risks on the path to improving your personal brand. Risk taking is an essential element of business and branding. Challenge yourself every day and set new goals to be accomplished. Setting daily targets for your personal brand is important. The target could be content related or aimed at audience building. In the same vein, ensure that there is a regular improvement in the quality of your brand. One way to grow your personal brand is to improve each day. Grow your area of expertise. If you started at a certain level, try to go some steps higher. There is always room for growth and learning. Substandard personal brands will be left in the dust by other competing brands.

Your Personal Branding Goals

Before developing your personal brand, you need to write out certain goals to achieve.

Your goals should be bold. Don't be afraid to set high goals. One factor that causes failure in personal branding is fear. It could be a fear of taking risks, fear of adapting to new things or fear of setting high goals. However, do not let this common fear overcome you. Initially, it might seem like you're overreaching, but in time you will find yourself achieving those set goals and even more. When setting your personal branding goals, pick out the ones that seem most daring. You'll find that those are the goals that are easily accomplished. However, your goals should also be realistic. Ensure that the goals you've set would be attainable within a period. Endeavor to set specific goals. Your goals should not be general or vague. As an example, instead of saying something like: "I want to have a large Twitter audience in the near future," say something like this instead:

- "I want to have a Twitter audience of about one hundred thousand followers by the end of the year."

- Create concrete goals. Your goals should be solid and not weak. Try to have a support system for your goals. It is quite brave to be a one-man army, but if you have a support system grab onto it for dear life.

- Have a defined method of working towards the achievement of your personal branding goals. Do not just set goals without having a plan. What are the strategies you can employ towards attaining your goals? Define those.

- Set a time target or deadline for the achievement of your goals. It could be within months or a year or two. At the end of the set time, analyze your personal brand and see how many of the goals you have achieved so far.

- How can you achieve your set goals within the designated period? It's quite simple. You need to act. No matter how minuscule or insignificant your actions seem, don't stop acting. Take tiny steps daily towards achieving your set goals.

- Always have a plan. If your plan fails, make sure you have a backup plan set in place.

With the right amount of determination and planning, you can achieve your personal branding goals within your deadline.

What Should Your Personal Brand Accomplish?

Every brand has a set goal, so your personal brand should be no different. Your brand should be relevant and add value to your audience. People follow personal brands in order to learn and gain valuable insight from them. If your personal brand has not impacted anyone positively or is not adding value to your followers, then you need to strategize anew. You can add value to your audience by providing them with vital information and tips on your area of expertise. Sharing your experiences on your journey to personal branding could also impact them positively and create relevance.

Your personal brand should equally tell your story to your audience. It should reflect your true self and everything you stand for—your values, ideas, and beliefs. Your personal brand must adequately reflect all these elements and present them favorably.

Your personal brand should build relationships between you and your audience and other brands. Relationship building is essential in all dimensions of branding. This is because the right relationships help to grow your brand. When you build a relationship with your audience, you encourage brand loyalty and referrals. Building a relationship with other competing brands would equally give you a platform to learn more and meet influential people who would help you grow your personal brand.

Your personal brand must be unique. It shouldn't adopt the status quo. If you want your personal brand to be unique, you must affix unusual features to it. What are other brands doing that you can do differently? A step to making your personal brand unique is by making use of bold, colorful visual representations. Any graphic design or picture that you upload on your website or social media handles should be of high quality and with a unique style.

Finally, your personal brand must achieve trust. You should be able to earn the trust of your audience and customers with your personal brand. Ensure that your brand is credible and trustworthy. Once you have gained those two qualities, ensure that your brand maintains that standard.

Chapter 3:
Find Your Niche

Having a strong personal brand is essential. However, your personal brand should not be a photocopy of another brand. It should have its own unique identity and should stand out. To achieve this, you need to identify your personal brand niche. You need to brainstorm and define your own niche.

How Do You Discover Your Personal Brand Niche?

Your niche is your specialty. It is your area of expertise. A niche is not something you can copy from other people. Everyone has a niche and you just need to discover yours. Finding your niche can be quite confusing as you might be talented at several things. However, there are certain steps you can take towards discovering your niche:

The first step is to lay down all the ideas that come into to mind. It might be a jumbled mess but write them down, anyway. These ideas should be your vision—what do you want to be known for? What exactly do you want to do? Your mission—why do you want to create a personal brand? What is your purpose? It should also include your goals— what do you want to achieve? It is important for you to establish your personal vision, values, and goals because if you have these, you will know the exact message you want to give, where you want to go and how to reach your destination. Even more so, it will help you see where there are opportunities that fit in with your visions. Also, it will help you from going on a path that is contrary to your goals. You will have set your priorities right by doing this. Then, write out your passions and where they fit. Your passions are what you love doing the most. They should be things that bring a spurt of joy to your heart, and what you love to do even without being paid. Make sure these are things you won't get tired of; things you'd still be doing in the next five to ten years without tiring. Your passions could be anything: golfing, beaching, writing, singing or any other thing you have a flair for. After this, the next thing you should do is to write down a list of all the skills you have acquired so far in life. This can be done by making a breakdown of all the places you have worked, the experiences you have gathered over the years in going about and doing your job. Was there a program you did about something you were interested in? Were you the best writer or vocalist in college? What do people commend you so much for? Write them down, alongside the knowledge you gained and other training, workshops, certifications, credentials, and awards you have received over the years. All these are necessary because they add to the pile of ideas and can help you locate where you fit in.

The next step is to analyze and reflect on all that you have written so far. As stated in previous chapters, your personal brand must add value to make it stand out. Thus, your niche must be one that attaches value to your person and your personal brand as well. Identify the skills that would be of either economic or intellectual value to you and select them. If any of your passions can create value for your brand, include it in the list too. One secret to finding your niche is to focus. What exactly do you want? Focusing on what you deem as important and deleting the irrelevant details will save you from drifting onto the wrong path, and help you create a brand to be proud of.

After you have followed the steps above, you need to ask yourself some crucial questions and provide answers to them. Ask yourself the following questions:

What area do you have the most experience in? What is it that I've done, or have taken interest in over the years? Experience is a determining factor in discovering your niche. You must be experienced in a field before you can build a personal brand around it.

How dedicated are you to your passion? Is it something that easily bores you? Is it something you can do for twenty hours without wanting to quit? Is it something you can do happily for the next couple of years? Can you do it anytime you are called to do so? You can be passionate about a thing without being dedicated to it. However, personal branding requires a certain level of dedication before it can thrive. Thus, you need to be dedicated to your passion.

Is there an existing market for your passions and skills? To find this, you must surf the net, a kind of market research. Conducting market research is very important, as it will help you know the target market, the demographic representation, and tastes of the existing market. If you discover that there is no market for your passions and skills, then you need to do an honest appraisal of yourself and your passions. That there is no existing market does not mean that there is no demand and use for your passions and skills. Now, you must ask yourself if you can create a market for what you are passionate about, using the skills that you have acquired over the years. Your passion and skills need to have an audience or market waiting for them, and if there is none, then you should figure out how to create one. If you try, and then realize that a market cannot be built around your passion or skills, then you need to drop the whole idea because it has no real value or use.

If your passion has value, and after asking and answering these crucial questions, and locating a market for your skills and passions, the final stage involves using all the information you gathered in the first three steps to determine your niche. Your niche is the area in which you have the most experience, and you are most passionate about. Only a true self-assessment will help you pinpoint your niche.

Now that you have defined your niche, your next mission should be to draft your personal brand's story. Your brand's story should be based upon your background, niche, tenets, and values. What are your most important core values? What do you believe in? What do you stand for and against?

What Should Your Personal Brand Be About?

Your personal brand is a narrative of yourself and how you want the world to see you. Having established this, your personal brand should contain your character, values, and ideas. It is basically an online representation of yourself. Your personal brand tells your story to the world. Your experiences, challenges, victories, and success story should all be reflected in your personal brand. For example, if someone wants to gain more information about you or what you do, the person simply must assess your personal brand. Thus, your personal brand should be about the best version of yourself.

A personal brand involves what you have to offer to the world and your target audience. It should have a story and be able to tell that story well. The purpose of a personal brand story is to connect and tap into your audience's emotions. Your story should be unique and coherent. It needs to give your audience an idea about your persona and keep them engaged as well.

Your personal brand should be about your special abilities. Identify your uniqueness and strengths. What makes you stand out? Learn your uniqueness and perfect your strengths. Read, absorb and create. It might be tempting to try to master the different skills that you have learned, all at the same time for the benefit of your personal brand, but it isn't advisable. Simply highlight your special skills and strengths and try to make them as memorable as possible.

Inasmuch as your personal brand should be all about you and your abilities, you should know when to apply discretion. Advertise your niche instead of your brand. Your audience does not need to know everything about you. Keep the sensitive details of your personal brand to yourself and give out the ones your audience needs.

Tips to Make Your Personal Brand Stand Out

Always choose your words carefully. Words can convey a million ideas at once. Beautifully written brand statements and content can make your brand seem different from the others. If you're doing something different, then be sure to look and sound different. No one would think that your brand is different or even better if you imitate other brands. If you must be remarkable, then go all the way, challenge yourself, and apply a unique style in your content creation. For example, content written in a storytelling or a memoir format would make your personal brand unique. Assuming sixty other similar brands create content revolving around photography in a descriptive way, you can make your content a refreshing experience for your audience by employing the narrative method. For example:

"Pictures, they say, are worth a thousand words. A picture taken at the right angle, however, is worth a hundred thousand more. Tracy discovered this fact the day she was jilted... "

By beginning your content this way, you have already hooked your audience and placed a distinguishing bar between your personal brand and other brands.

Another way of creating uniqueness for your personal brand is to challenge yourself by taking risks. Staying within your comfort zone would only result in your personal brand being average and generic. To stand out, you need to take risks that other competing brands wouldn't think of taking. Set a new target for yourself every day and beat those targets.

A unique brand needs a distinctive online presence. This implies that your online presence must be strong enough to boost your brand. Make your brand successful on the relevant social media platforms. Your social media accounts should be used to build relationships and generate trust between your personal brand and your audience. You can boost your online presence by being constantly active, developing great content and employing crucial social media tools.

Create your own branding style. Be yourself and find what suits you. You don't have to do what every other person is doing because of the gains they are making from it. Do not follow the crowd, as it would lead you to nowhere near success and perfection. It will only make you leave your priorities to chase what is already circulated. Rather, use your style and uniqueness to attract what you want. Let your style be so remarkable that it will be easily differentiated from the rest. Having identified yourself, your values, and set your priorities, you will have a clearer picture of your personal and professional goals both long term and short term. This helps to make your style unique. It serves as a compass that guides you both in the actions and tasks you will carry out and helps you in making the right decisions that will propel your brand to greater heights. Another thing that works in sync to give your style an edge is your "voice." It is very important that you find your voice. Sit down, think deeply and reflect. Your voice is one of the most important things in creating your branding style. For instance, if you are a passionate literature writer, then your voice lives on literary papers. On another hand, if you are a guitarist, your voice lives on in the melodies you produce. This voice should be structured and organized in a way that can be easily differentiated and recognized from the many other voices that abound.

Watch your manners. Mannerisms affect the brand and content in a great way. Are you snobbish? Do you maintain a static opinion even when it's unpopular? Do you use vulgar and discriminatory words? If you want your brand to stand out, you should pay attention to your manners. This does not mean that you should have no opinions at all; rather, it helps you keep check of what you say and do. Related to mannerism is the need to revisit your habits. Are your habits slowing down the progress of your brand? Does your audience have reservations about your habits as reflected in your contents?

Keep your word. Many brands out there create a false persona to attract a large community. Don't do this—remember that you shouldn't follow the crowd. Be true to yourself, and do not say what you cannot do. If you make promises, try your best and see that you fulfill them before the deadline. No one wants to waste their time with a brand that continuously fails them. The audience knows where to get whatever they want, but they need to select from brands that they can trust, and trust comes only when you keep your word.

Be consistent. As much as possible, try to be very consistent. Keep generating new content that will keep your audience engaged. The more engaged they are, the most likely it is that they will never get bored with your brand. Of course, as discussed earlier, since your brand reflects your interests, what you are passionate about, and the skills you have learned over the years, it would be only natural for you to enjoy doing it and sticking with your goals for many more years to come. This directly and positively affects your wealth of experience and brand.

Make your brand and content irresistible. Do not create your brand in a way that would make the target audience see it like other brands. This can be done by staying original and offering great content with the best quality. There is the need to combine the things you love doing, the ones you do best, and the ones your audience want but do not get. When these three elements blend into your content and brand, then be sure that you have perfectly carved a niche for yourself and will always be easily differentiated from the other brands. Since the audience cannot now do without your brand, as they have discovered what suits their taste, they will flock to it and stay active because your niche has given them what they want. You will then enjoy perhaps the largest audience and community in the market.

Chapter 4:
Why YouTube Should Be Your First Step

If you are trying to develop your personal brand, the first thing you should do is to create a YouTube channel. Why should YouTube be your first step? YouTube is a very popular search engine. As a matter of fact, it is ranked number two right after Google. If you want your personal brand to be popular, you must be on every platform that has the highest user demographic. YouTube boasts of millions of users who drift through the platform for different categories of videos. Every day, people search through YouTube for videos that suit their interests. Often, they stumble upon random videos that might not be within their area of interest, but they might like those videos and want to see more from that brand. Therefore, you need to be on YouTube.

YouTube gives you the opportunity to showcase your brand in not just written form but in video format too. It creates room for exploring and testing your limits and hidden skills. On YouTube, you get the chance to impress your target audience with your speaking and presentation skills. For personal brand owners who have little or no writing skills, you can easily make up for those deficiencies on

YouTube. All you must do is to post high-quality videos and convey your message concisely.

People love to watch videos, and there is a high chance of users stumbling upon your YouTube content and joining your audience. Most social media users prefer visual representations to written format. Thus, you can easily build a following on YouTube if you understand how it works.

As a personal brand, you need to create an audience on YouTube first before moving on to other platforms. This is because YouTube builds your confidence as a person and as a brand. With YouTube, you learn to get in front of a camera without fear or shyness. Also, you learn how to communicate your ideas and knowledge to your audience coherently. As stated in previous chapters, every personal brand needs to add value to the audience. YouTube creates a perfect opportunity for you to do so.

YouTube is quite valuable to your personal brand. It helps to promote brand growth by regularly driving subscribers to your channel. It gives your personal brand exposure as it has a wider outreach than most other platforms.

Furthermore, it builds credibility. A popular saying goes, "Seeing is believing." Your target audience is more likely to believe the authenticity of your personal brand if they can see the level of your knowledge and expertise for themselves, especially in video format.

Having a YouTube channel gives your brand a mark of professionalism. Every top professional has a YouTube channel where they showcase their skills and give tutorials. YouTube puts you on the same level as those professionals.

How You Can Use YouTube To Improve Your Personal Brand

YouTube can greatly improve your personal brand if utilized correctly. Before developing your personal brand on YouTube, you need to clearly define what your brand is. What is going to be your niche on YouTube? How well can you handle your personal brand?

Advertise your personal brand on YouTube. Define and carve your niche and announce it to your target audience. Do not confuse your audience by changing niches. YouTube has certain elements that could boost your personal brand. First, it gives you exposure and connects you to your target audience.

It should be noted that on YouTube, there is an order. Videos should be posted in a progression, and not all at once. You can divide a video into sections, then shoot and post each section at intervals. You can use YouTube to boost your personal brand by following basic strategies for success.

How Do You Get Started on YouTube?

The first stage of developing your personal brand on YouTube is to create a profile and brand it. You can start by making a short introductory video of yourself and your brand. This is your introduction to your target audience, and it should be professional and impressionable.

The next step is to create a name for your channel. It is always advisable to use a straightforward professional name. Set up your profile. YouTube has a myriad of themes and colors that you could use to liven up your videos.

Create a unique angle for your videos and channel. YouTube is home to millions of videos, and you will find yourself competing with those videos to make it to the top of the list. To find your unique angle, ask yourself some vital questions. What do you want for your brand? Do you want to tread the path of humor or entertainment? Find a way to make your videos unique and interesting, at least.

Always ensure that your videos are of high quality and include a link to your other social media platforms to ensure a wider outreach for your personal brand. Now, the key to developing your personal brand on YouTube is to have a strong YouTube presence. But how do you do that?

How to Create A Strong YouTube Presence?
The first step is to decide the kind of videos to make. The videos you post on YouTube must be related to your personal brand. Create a schedule for your posting. Decide if you are going to be posting weekly or bi-weekly. Endeavor to religiously follow this schedule you have set because your audience will be counting on you to be consistent with

your delivery. Try as much as possible to keep your videos short. Most social media users will not watch excessively long videos. Ideally, YouTube videos that won't bore your audience should be between five to eight minutes. Keep them short and simple.

Discover what would make your videos remarkable. Try to customize your channel. There are a lot of themes on YouTube that you could apply to your videos to give them a signature look. Giving your videos a signature look will help your audience to identify your brand whenever they see it. You could include a short, catchy intro video to help gain brand recognition and loyalty.

Promote all your YouTube videos by using optimized keywords. This would make it easier for your target audience to find your videos on YouTube. Understand SEO. Search Engine Optimization involves using the right keywords to find your desired results on the web. Pay attention to the YouTube algorithm and align your posts with it. You can equally partner with notable figures or experts within your niche. This would draw both your audience and their audience to your YouTube channel. Include a call to action at the end of all your videos to inspire your audience to share with their network of friends.

Share your YouTube videos on all your social media platforms. You have a different audience on each social media platform. Draw your Facebook, Twitter and Instagram audience to your YouTube channel.

You could drop the link to your YouTube channel on your other social media handles.

Increase the number of your subscribers. It's hard to build a strong YouTube presence if your list of subscribers is low. How do you increase your number of subscribers? First, stop listening to those ads that pop up and ask you to buy followers. To grow your list of subscribers, you need to stop thinking about hacks and possible ways to cheat the algorithm. What you need to do is to focus on putting in actual work and growing your subscribers organically. To do this, you need to feature other popular channels occasionally. This would draw people to your channel as they will want to see what you and their favorite brand have to say. If you keep them interested, they will subscribe to your channel. Also, note that success is very easy to tap into on YouTube. If you want to draw a flock of subscribers to your channel, search for trending videos on YouTube, and create a video around that. Your video could be an analysis of a popular video or simply an expansion of it. However, do not copy.

Another way to create a strong YouTube presence is by constantly engaging your audience in the comment section. Your audience might have a question or two to ask after watching your videos. Encourage them to ask their questions in the comment section and answer those questions. Audience engagement and interaction is a great boost to your YouTube presence.

You can monitor how your YouTube channel is doing. Scrutinize the analytics. YouTube analytics tell you how much progress you have made. It shows you a percentile representation of how much interaction you have had on your YouTube channel each week. It also shows which videos had the most interaction and the reactions of your audience to your videos.

Common Mistakes to Avoid on YouTube

A lot of new YouTubers and brands make some common easily avoidable mistakes. These mistakes could cause potential harm to your YouTube channel or personal brand. As a new brand seeking to expand your presence on YouTube, these are the mistakes you should avoid making.

Don't upload videos with poor audio quality. Your videos shouldn't just be of high quality; your audio should be too. Some YouTube videos are filled with so much background noise that you can barely hear what the YouTuber is saying. In some other videos, the YouTuber talks in such a low tone, you must strain or read his lips to understand what he's saying. These videos barely keep your audience engaged as they'll be put off by the poor audio quality of your video and will avoid any other content you upload in the future.

Some personal brands are in so much of a hurry to become successful or go viral on YouTube that they resort to buying fake, low-quality views on YouTube. The consequence of this mistake is that it eventually backfires on you. It is quite easy to fish out fake views on YouTube, and once your audience notices that you have been buying fake views, you lose their trust and your reputation.

Another mistake you should avoid is the urge tu move on to new things. A little diversity is great for your brand and channel, but when you leave your niche completely and move on to an entirely new niche, your audience which was interested in your original niche, will become disappointed and drop off.

As a personal brand, it is normal to want to drive more traffic to your channel and want more views. However, desist from constantly asking for views under other YouTubers' comment sections. For example, saying something like "Guys, please subscribe to my channel and see a lot of fun things" under another YouTuber's post about skincare. Not only would you annoy the YouTuber and his audience, but it is also unprofessional and paints your personal brand and your channel in a bad light. Finally, most personal brands make the mistake of not promoting their channels enough. Promote your channels on YouTube and other external platforms.

Strategies for Success on YouTube

YouTube success is not limited to having thousands of likes or followers. It also encompasses your true audience. Have you successfully created a loyal following? Does your audience love and recognize your brand? Here are some strategies to create YouTube success:

- Be professional. People want to know that you are an expert within your niche. You do not have to dress or speak formally to be professional. Simply stick to what you do and convey your ideas and concepts directly to your audience.

- Consistency is the key. Do not be hot and cold. Your audience is eagerly waiting to hear and learn from you. If there is any reason for a delay in posting your content, inform your audience and sign off with a sincere apology.

- Resist the urge to constantly attempt to sell yourself. Focus more on teaching and impacting your audience positively than selling. Your audience needs to know that they can trust you. If you're constantly trying to sell yourself to them, you might send the wrong message.

- Don't be afraid of adapting. New trends and innovations are being churned out daily. It's all a part of risk-taking and in branding; risk-taking is essential.

- Have a prepared script to work with. However, this doesn't mean that you should sound uptight in your videos or read from a script. You should have a script guiding you as to what to say in your videos. This is to avoid making constant mistakes and having to re-shoot your videos.

- Endeavor to deliver top-notch content regularly. Your videos should be of high quality and something your audience can learn from. The fastest way to kill your YouTube presence is by producing substandard content.

- As a personal brand, do not make yourself look like a corporation. Your audience wants to feel friendliness and warmth from you. Do not be stiff or overly formal in your videos. Instead, try to effuse warmth as opposed to formality.

- Always edit and re-edit your videos before putting them out there. Do not overlook any errors because they seem insignificant or harmless. Your videos need to be seamless, so keep editing until you have the perfect video.

- Network and collaborate with other personal brands within your niche. Create partnerships and relationships with other brands on YouTube. This will put you on the map and attract more subscribers to your channel.

- Have a catchphrase or a branding statement. This will help to place insignia on your personal brand. Most popular YouTubers have a catchphrase which they are known for. Develop your catchphrase and use it in your videos. However, your catchphrase should not be overused as this would make it redundant. Use it just once or twice in each video.

- Constantly analyze your brand and the progress you've made so far. A great way to be successful is by constant analyzing and comparison. Compare the current state of your personal brand and YouTube channel to its previous state when you first began. Check for noticeable progress and keep pushing ahead.

The YouTube website gives your brand the right kind of exposure, and in the next chapter, we will be talking about the YouTube algorithm—how it works and how to beat it.

Chapter 5:
Exposing the YouTube Algorithm

The YouTube algorithm is the AI behind how YouTube works. It is responsible for driving traffic towards YouTube videos that it deems relevant to increase their views. For a video to be considered suitable by the YouTube algorithm, it must fulfill certain criteria. Most YouTubers do not understand how the algorithm works, and that is why some channels struggle to become successful on YouTube.

How the YouTube Algorithm Works

The YouTube algorithm drives traffic towards different videos after considering several factors. What the YouTube algorithm tries to achieve is to make sure that the most relevant videos are brought to the forefront. Thus, when you type in a keyword, the algorithm produces the most relevant videos related to that keyword. This mostly builds a high video reach. Your impressions determine your video reach. Impressions are simply how many times your video thumbnail was displayed on the YouTube website to its users. It is important to note that not all impressions are considered impressions by the YouTube algorithm. For example, if someone saw your video thumbnail through external links such as other social media platforms or emails, it wouldn't be counted. Thus, what you think is an impression might not really count as an impression.

Do you have a high impression rate on YouTube? Don't rejoice yet. Let's say you have an impression rate of about five hundred thousand people. The next thing to consider is your click-through rate. How many of those YouTubers who saw your video thumbnail clicked on it? Your click-through rate (CTR) is the total number of people who saw your video thumbnail and clicked on it. These are your viewers. If your click-through rate is high, the chances of your video appearing very frequently on people's home page or suggested videos increases. Most of the time, your CTR is lower than your impressions rate. This is because some YouTubers who come across your video might not be interested enough to click on it.

The next factor to consider is your watch time metric. Simply put, watch time is the average amount of time that viewers spend on your video. Watch time has to do with the amount of time a YouTuber spends watching your video. For example, if a viewer spends an hour on YouTube, what percentage of that time is spent watching your video(s)? If a viewer spends about half of his or her YouTube session watching your video(s), then your watch time metric increases and the algorithm would conclude that your video is relevant, and your content would begin to pop up more on YouTube.

The YouTube algorithm also considers audience retention. Your audience retention is the percentage of time people spend watching your video. For instance, if you upload a video that is ten minutes long on YouTube and the average amount of time people spend on your video is three minutes, then your audience retention is about 30 percent. Most times, YouTube users do not watch videos to the end. They watch a certain percentage, and then they move on to other videos. The algorithm is interested in your audience retention. For how long can you keep your audience hooked and entertained? When your audience retention is at a high percentage, the algorithm considers it relevant and you'd begin to have a broader outreach. That is, if your video is interesting enough to keep your audience watching till the end or at least a significant amount of time, then your video becomes relevant on YouTube.

Where Does the Algorithm Place Your Videos?

ONCE YOUR VIDEO has a high click-through rate, watch time metric, and audience retention, it begins to appear more frequently on YouTube. The first place your video pops up on is the search bar or search results. When you type in a keyword, the YouTube algorithm brings up the videos most relevant to that keyword. For your video to show up on the search results, the algorithm considers specific criteria. The algorithm considers the YouTuber's viewing history and your video's tags, captions and so on.

Your video is also placed under suggested videos for viewers. When a YouTube user watches a video, YouTube often recommends a related video. What the algorithm does here is that it tries to determine what the viewer would like to see next. Suggested or recommended videos are usually connected to the video last watched by the viewer. That is, they are often within the same niche. Suggested videos are often placed based on different criteria. Most times, the algorithm considers the user's interests and recent activities.

- What kind of content does the user like to see?

- What has been the user's preference in recent times?

- What channels has the user subscribed to recently?

The algorithm considers this before showing suggested videos. It tries to suggest videos that are aligned with the criteria listed above. Also, the algorithm scrutinizes video ratings. How high does your video rank on YouTube? These are also taken into consideration. Video descriptions, captions, tags and thumbnails equally determine whether your video would pop up under suggested videos.

As a personal brand, your video can also appear on YouTube's home page. However, this is quite difficult and can only happen if your video has gone viral or is trending. How do you make your video go viral?

The first step to creating a potentially viral video is to create high-quality content. For your video to go viral, it must be something viewers would love and enjoy watching. The next step is to utilize SEO tools. Use great keywords, tags and have a good video description. Develop the right strategies, and in no time your video will be viral.

The YouTube algorithm also places your videos under viewers' notifications. When YouTube users update their settings to get notifications from some of their favorite or subscribed channels, these videos pop up in their notifications. If you're lucky enough, your personal brand might impress your audience so much that they'd want to get notifications when you upload new content. For example, if a viewer likes a previous video of yours, he/she would look forward to seeing more content from you and would update his notification settings. Thus, your videos would begin to show up in his notifications.

The final place where the algorithm places your videos is in the news feed of your subscribers. A subscriber is a "fan" of your personal brand and content. When a user falls in love with your personal brand, he would want to stay updated on what you do. Thus, he would subscribe to your channel to get more updates and content from you.

Viral Content; Why Do Some Videos Trend More Than Others?

Trending or viral videos on YouTube are basically videos that have a high number of likes, views, and ratings. YouTube has a trending category where it places videos that are currently trending. YouTube trending videos are not constant. This means that a video trending today might not be trending anymore within the next four or five hours. Trending videos on YouTube include videos that have a high number of views, videos that are sensational, or new or videos that appeal to many YouTube users.

Now, to the million-dollar question: What makes certain videos on YouTube trend more than others?

The critical factor in getting a YouTube video to trend is content. You want your personal brand to grow and reach all the nooks and crannies of YouTube. Develop good content. Every viral video on YouTube has great content (either educational or humorous) that keeps viewers hooked to the very end.

Another element that makes videos trend on YouTube is the content data. Content data includes Search Engine Optimization tools. YouTube channels that create viral videos have taken advantage of this powerful tool. High ranking keywords can make your video go viral. However, ensure that the keyword does not have excessive competition. For instance, if you analyze a keyword and you realize that it brings up about fifteen million results, abort the mission. Using keywords with a high level of competition may cause your video not to trend because your video would be hidden under millions of videos that have the same keywords. So, what do you do? Try to create a variation or unique keyword. Similarly, videos with catchy titles and descriptions go viral easier than others.

As stated earlier, watch time metric plays a huge role in whether a video becomes viral or not. Videos with a high percentage of watch time metric, get pushed up to YouTube's trending charts. If you want your video to go viral, you need to be mindful of time. Upload your content at specific times when people would be more likely to take interest in it and watch it.

What Should You Focus On?

As a personal brand struggling to achieve success on YouTube, there are certain things you should focus on to get your brand where you want it to be. Most new channels focus on the wrong things and don't make any progress on YouTube.

The most important thing for you to place your focus on is your audience. Your audience should be your priority. Don't focus on how many views or subscribers you wish you had. Focus on what your audience is interested in and how to build your personal brand on YouTube around those interests. To do this, you must analyze your past content. Which videos did you have the most audience interaction on? Analyze the content of those videos, and it may give you a clue as to what your audience really wants to see from you. Secondly, focus on engaging your audience and boosting audience engagement. If you are not satisfied with the number of comments you get per post, try to include questions or topics that would generate questions or comments from your audience.

As a personal brand, you should really focus on your content. Your content is what makes or breaks your brand. To thrive on YouTube, you need to create engaging and entertaining content. Your content should revolve around topics that you are well-versed in to show your audience that you know what you are doing. Do not churn out half-baked content or upload videos that are blurry or of poor camera quality. Scrutinize your videos with a professional eye before uploading them.

To make your brand successful on YouTube, you need to focus on your audience or viewers retention. It's not just about uploading content regularly. What would be the point of uploading regularly if your audience doesn't even care enough to listen to what you have to say? Monitor and analyze your audience retention. If it is not satisfactory, devise new strategies for improving your audience retention. In subsequent parts of this chapter, you will learn how to boost your audience retention. If you create a fifteen- minute video and most of your audience watch at least half of the video, then you have greatly improved your audience retention.

Another aspect you should focus on is promotion. One of the tenets of personal branding is promotion or marketing. How well do you promote your brand? Do you focus solely on content and then leave your brand to promote itself? If you do not promote your brand, no one else will. Promote your brand to the extent of your capabilities.

Encourage your subscribers to share your content with their network of friends. Share links to your YouTube channel on other social media platforms. Include calls to action within your videos and in your annotations.

Most importantly, focus on learning the intricacies of Search Engine Optimization. This will help give your YouTube channel and content the exposure you desire. The YouTube algorithm is there to help if you know how to use it to your advantage.

How to Increase Your Click-Through Rate?

As stated earlier, your impressions click-through rate is the number of users who come across your video thumbnail anywhere on YouTube and decide to click on the video (i.e. view it).

Now, how do you increase your click-through rate? How do you persuade many YouTubers to watch your video when they see your video thumbnail? To increase your click-through rate, you need to have a very attractive, eye-catching, and unique video thumbnail. On YouTube, your video thumbnail is what introduces viewers to the content you have just uploaded. As such, it should stand out. Large, colorful words should be used. The picture on your video thumbnail should be something that would compel the viewer to click on your video. In order to know what your video thumbnail should look like;

you need to study your user demographic. Know the age and gender percentile of YouTube users and try to create a video thumbnail around their interests and preferences.

Have a very catchy title. Improve the way you title your videos and content. If you have been attaching generic titles to your videos on YouTube, you need to improve them immediately. More thought should be put into titling your videos. For example, imagine a video title:

"How makeup can transform your face."

It seems like a good enough title for your video. Now, imagine a video title like this:

"Top ten makeup tricks that can take you from 0-100."

You would find the second video title catchier and more appealing, and you'd be more likely to click on the second video rather than the first even though they have the same content.

How to Increase Your Audience Retention?

There are basically two types of audience retention. They are absolute audience retention and relative audience retention. Your total audience retention is the overall ratio between the number of viewers watching your video at the beginning and the number of viewers at later parts of the video. On the other hand, your relative audience retention is the number of viewers that stay hooked to your video compared to the audience retention of other videos with a similar length.

One way to improve your audience retention is to analyze and critique your past videos. You can make use of YouTube analytics to do this. Try to discover the point at which most of your viewers dropped off and work on those parts. Try to reduce the length of your videos. It's quite tempting to say everything you want to say and make a long video, but your viewers would probably get bored at some point. Make your videos shorter. Make your content visually engaging and entertaining. The truth is, most viewers will likely move on to other videos after the first fifteen seconds. The more entertaining your video is, the less likely they would be to drop off.

Finally, compare your video with your other videos to gauge how your audience retention has either improved or dropped. To get the most out of YouTube, focus on relevant things and keep improving daily.

Chapter 6:
What Instagram Can Do for You

Instagram is a veritable platform for personal brand growth and development. In this chapter, you will learn the value of Instagram for your personal brand and how you can use this social media network to your advantage.

The Value of Instagram For Personal Branding

The entire landscape of businesses and brands have changed over the past few years. Before now, brands focused on guerilla marketing strategies to get and keep their customers. This usually translated to spending a lot of money on advertisements, on TV and radio stations and often, smaller brands found themselves struggling to keep up with the bigger fish in the pond. However, fast forward to the present and we find that the adoption of the internet, especially social media platforms such as Instagram and Twitter have completely evened out the playing field.

Instagram, especially, has proved to be a very powerful tool for personal branding. With over seven hundred million users monthly, it can be a springboard for brands to put themselves out there and solidify their value in the minds of their consumers and target customers. The importance of this is reinforced by the fact that about 50 percent of consumers hint that they consider becoming loyal to a brand during their first purchase or impression. Thus, what better way to put your brand out there than to do so on a platform that guarantees that over half a billion users have a chance of seeing you? It should be noted that Instagram is a profoundly visual platform. Before going into Instagram as a tool to help you grow your brand, it is essential to know that branding is aimed not just at accomplishing the usual task of getting your prospective customers to prefer you over your competitors. Branding aims at positioning yourself as a leader in your market, as an entity which continually addresses the issues or problems of its audience, while connecting with your audience on an emotional level.

The ability of the Instagram platform to help achieve this lies in the sheer number of content-hungry users it boasts of daily. The statistics to support its influence on these users are there for all to see and some of them include:

As much as 20 percent of Instagram users are known to buy a product or lay into a brand they exclusively know or found on Instagram. Seven out of ten hashtags on Instagram are branded, and each post accommodates thirty hashtags. In the same vein, more than fifty-five million photos are actively shared by Instagram users daily.

Instagram boasts a daily usage of five hundred million users. The best feature about this social network is that the platform is not only beneficial to B2C or C2B markets but even as much of a value to B2B companies. Just about anyone can produce relevant visual experiences for their target audience to consume, thus solidifying their brand experience while making sales at the same time. Remember, previous polls show that 70 percent of Instagram users report having looked up a brand on the Instagram platform. Hence, you may want to utilize Instagram as much as you can.

How to Get Started on Instagram

Statistics show that small and medium-sized enterprises (SMEs) are hesitant in using Instagram for their businesses, and this could be mainly attributed to the fear of the unknown, or the reluctance associated with leaving their comfort zones. For some, the idea of having to invest time and money into a platform online is a risk too big to take, more so if such brands are service-based as opposed to product-based brands. However, if your brand can provide catchy visuals, then you can leverage the Instagram platform and all its marketing potential.

As you would have already guessed by now, starting up on Instagram begins when you decide to open an Instagram account for your personal brand. Try to use the same username that you would want your business or brand to be associated with when opening your Instagram account. However, in the case where another Instagram user has already used your proposed name, you can add a few special characters such as underscores and period marks to ensure that you get set up without losing the identity of the brand in the process. You may choose to open a business account on the Instagram platform to enable you to track your analytics better and use the results to channel your posts and resources or ads to where they would be most effective. If you already have an Instagram account set up, but under a personal profile, you could always convert it to a business profile in a few steps on the platform.

The next important factor to take note of when setting up your brand's Instagram account is the importance of backlinks. Here, we are focusing on leading users directly to your personal website or personal page. Your bio is the one place in Instagram where your link is clickable, and you should utilize that opportunity as much as you can. It is located under your name at the top of your Instagram profile.

The bio of your Instagram profile is a part where most Instagram users go before deciding to follow your page or move on to the next brand. Thus, it is highly advisable that you get the best out of it. Ensure that you use a catchy and informative bio and typically avoid descriptions that make it seem like you have a robot operating your account. People tend to gravitate towards things or places that seem welcoming. Hence, you should add a human factor to your bio as it would go a long way in making them stay. Convince them in a few words about the value which your personal brand would add to their feed if they were to click the follow button. Do not forget to include your brand name, a description of your brand, and a link to your personal website. Your Instagram bio should effectively tell your audience what your brand is all about. You can always change your bio if you need to. For example, if you upload new content on YouTube or your personal website, you can update your bio and include the link to the content.

Tips for Creating the Ideal Personal Brand on Instagram

After taking the first steps to set up an Instagram account for your brand, it is important to do certain things that may help you get ahead in creating the ideal brand image in the minds of your Instagram audience.

Create appealing posts based on what your audience wants to see. Every brand has certain traits or ideas that endear users. It is advised that you carefully study the behavioral patterns of your audience based on the analytics and feedback from your earlier posts and from other similar brands within your niche. Knowing your audience will help greatly as you prepare posts that you are certain they would be eager to pay attention to.

Use creative and crisp looking high-resolution images. Instagram is an image-centric platform, and thus, the type and quality of images used will heavily influence the image of any brand looking to leverage on its capabilities. Nowadays, social media users have mobile devices with improved technologies such as HD screens and QHD displays, all aimed at enhancing their viewing experience all around. In that same vein, no smartphone user would want to spend thousands of dollars on a high-end phone, only to view blurry images. They would rather move on to the next brand with more visually appealing content, even if it offers less than the former in terms of captions.

Even on other social media platforms such as Facebook, posts containing an image usually get twice as much engagement than ordinary posts uploaded with no picture or video attached to them. Harness the visual-based appeal of Instagram and create photos or animations that will keep your audience's attention on your post for more than just a couple of seconds.

If your brand is product-based, high-resolution photos of your products will be essential in determining conversion rates on your Instagram. This is because about 67 percent of consumers consider crisp photos to be more appealing and persuasive towards making their purchase. This number of respondents surpass those who feel the caption or description of the product is the key determinant in their purchases. Visuals help you show your products without hard selling them.

Keep your posts tied to the image or persona your brand wants to create in the minds of your audience. One thing you should avoid on Instagram and any other social network, is contradiction. Brand

loyalists remain so because they know what to expect from their preferred brands. Otherwise, there would be no brand loyalty. One creative way to achieve this is by creating content that possess the human appeal irrespective of whatever it is that your brand is known
for. Show off your personality in your post. Most personal brands
have utilized this life hack. They know that consumers nowadays don't
just buy the product; they buy the idea behind the product.

Tell stories with your posts. Irrespective of what your brand stands
for, you can always find a short story to create from your ideas. Even
things as simple as behind the scenes cuts can get your audience
hooked on your page. Simply put, the modern-day consumer buys stories. Give them loads of them.

Create content offering your followers advice around your areas of
strength. Your consumers want to be entertained as much as they
want to be guided. Finding a way to fuse these two desires of your
audience into your posts is guaranteed to produce results.

Promote your services or products. After filling your consumers in
with the catchy contents you have to offer, you would not want to
forget to keep them updated about the services and products you
have in store for them. Remember to make these posts creative as
well so that they do not move sharply from feeling entertained by your
brand to feeling overwhelmed with your promotions.

Finally, tie it all together. By this, it is advised to post on your Instagram page with consistency. Be consistent with your time of posting content and style of posts. The goal is to ensure that if a new visitor comes to your Instagram profile and looks at it, in a few seconds, they should be able to grasp what kind of brand you are and what to expect from following you. If they make the jump from your Instagram feed to your website or landing page, it should be clear to them that both platforms belong to the same brand.

Is Instagram The Right Social Media Platform for Your Personal Brand?

This is the big question brand managers ask themselves when considering the need to open an Instagram account for their personal brand, and rightfully so. It is true that the Instagram platform services a wide range of brands and businesses and that irrespective of the brand's position, it can benefit from having an Instagram presence. It is also true that certain kinds of businesses or brands tend to stand out more on other platforms apart from Instagram. This is especially true for brands that rely heavily on captions, texts and generally text-based businesses and brands. If your brand is a B2B, you may want to consider a twitter account to go with your Instagram page, as this better allows you to interact directly with your customers and other businesses without the added flair of pictures and images. Twitter is basically for every kind of brand but requires more regular updates and posts in order to maintain relevance as it is a largely interactive platform. Your brand can start or join conversations at will and post as many times per day as you find relevant. Additionally, you have certain tools that help with your Twitter account management, such as scheduling content to post even when you are not actively operating the Twitter account.

If your business is a B2B service provider, then you may also need to have a LinkedIn account or profile. This is especially true for job recruiters and research-based companies. The recommended posting frequency is not as much as that of Twitter or even Instagram, and you can opt for the use of longer text material as opposed to the visuals you would like on Instagram.

Facebook is also a good platform for building your personal brand but with the recent change in the Facebook algorithm that determines how much of a brand or business content is being shown on the timelines of individuals and the heavily-monetized process of posting ads, more and more brands are unwilling to solidify their presence on Facebook nowadays. However, if you have a good digital marketer who knows the best methods to target your ads, then you should use the platform. Facebook offers personal connections and the ability to track the success of your content by date and time to determine the best times to interact with your users or consumers.

At this point, the importance of using the Instagram platform to promote personal brands cannot be overlooked. Every day, a great percentage of the younger generation log into their Instagram account hungry for content, and they are never satisfied. What you must do is to prepare your brand and use their insatiable need to be entertained as leverage.

Since 2014, there has been a decline in the reach of the information-heavy articles and write-ups as these methods gave way to the rise of visual-heavy content. People now see the increased level of brand engagement they potentially could gain if they switch to image-based communication, and a lot of brands are adjusting. People nowadays have shorter attention spans and need content or stimulation fast and Instagram is the first platform they go to get satisfaction.

It is important, however, to heed the tips for building your personal brand on Instagram, or you may risk using up precious time, brainpower and resources without seeing any positive feedback or return from the energy you have spent. An example of what to avoid doing on Instagram is creating last-minute content. The post you create in the last seconds of your working day is probably not going to be your best. As a matter of fact, it may end up undoing all your hard work because you are more likely to create sub-par content. That is, content that does not align with the brand's image and values, and you can be sure that your audience would notice these slip-ups.

It is advisable to create a posting plan for your Instagram profile and keep to it judiciously, tracking your audience's behavioral patterns using the inbuilt Instagram analytics. This way, you make certain that the posts you put up for your target audience endear them towards identifying with your personal brand and creating a base of brand-loyalists to call your own.

Chapter 7:
The Instagram Algorithm to Dominate

The Instagram algorithm is responsible for arranging and sorting posts from different Instagram users into an order. The algorithm uses a reverse-chronological order to rank and display posts.

However, the problem with the Instagram algorithm is that it displays your posts to only a tiny percentage of your Instagram followers. For instance, if you make an Instagram post, only between 10-15 percent of your followers might see that post. An even smaller percentage will like or comment on the post. This explains why you might have a large following, but your likes don't match your audience.

What the algorithm is trying to do is to decipher the amount of engagement you have on your posts. The higher the engagement, the higher your posts will be ranked. If most of the 10-15 percent of people who saw your post liked and commented on it, the Instagram algorithm would conclude that your post is relevant and begin to show it to a wider percentage of your followers. Thus, the key to getting a broader reach on Instagram is by constant engagement. When you have continuous engagement on your Instagram account, the algorithm will begin to suggest your account to other Instagram users.

One common misconception about the Instagram algorithm is that most people think it hides posts and that your Instagram post can only be unhidden or revealed when you pay for ads or constantly engage. That isn't true. Instagram does NOT hide your posts. What it does is it ranks different posts on a priority scale and depending on how relevant it deems a post, presents them in order. Further sections of this chapter will explain what ranking factors the Instagram algorithm uses and how to get your posts to rank high. Here are some common myths about the Instagram algorithm:

The most common myth is the belief that Instagram hides your posts.

Another common myth among Instagram users is that the use of too many hashtags on your posts or comments would cause the algorithm to shadow ban you. Shadow banning means your hashtags are rendered invisible to other Instagram users apart from your followers, which completely trumps the purpose of hashtags. The use of numerous hashtags would not cause you to be shadow banned. However, it is advisable to use only relevant and powerful hashtags.

That top-ranking posts are the same for every Instagram user is another myth that needs to be debunked. The algorithm ranks posts differently for each user. It tries to note the user's preferences and ranks posts according to the user's preferences. It also ranks the posts according to the user's following (i.e. the accounts the user is following). Thus, posts can never be ranked the same way for all users.

Some Instagram users believe that the algorithm favors some functions more than the others. They feel that posting more Instagram stories as opposed to just making posts would earn them a wider reach. This is false. The algorithm does not favor any functions and posting stories instead of posts will not increase your reach.

Another myth is that switching or converting your account from a personal account to a business one would lower your reach. Switching from a personal account to a business account has no effect whatsoever on your reach. You might merely experience a shift in the type of audience that your account is exposed to.

Ranking Factors

What factors does the Instagram algorithm consider before ranking posts? The first factor the algorithm considers is the user's relationships with other accounts. When a user frequently likes, comments and interacts with another Instagram account, the algorithm begins to show them each other's posts more frequently. For example, if User A constantly interacts with User B on Instagram and vice versa, the algorithm would assume that they will find each other's posts relevant. Thus, User A's posts will begin to appear at the top of User B's news feed and vice versa. The stronger your online relationship is with other users, the higher your post ranking will be on their news feeds.

Another factor that the algorithm considers is the interests and preferences of the user. Based on the user's recent engagement, the algorithm determines the content the user prefers to see and will immediately begin to display more of that content, prioritizing it over others. For example, if you have recently been liking and commenting on fitness posts, the Instagram algorithm will begin to bring up content related to fitness. Similarly, if you have been interacting on posts relating to beauty and skincare, the algorithm will prioritize that content category for you and begin to show you beauty and skincare posts first.

The time frame of a post also determines its ranking on Instagram. How recent is your post? As stated earlier, the Instagram algorithm operates a reverse-chronological order. Thus, more recent posts are displayed before older posts. The older your post gets, the lower the algorithm ranks it. For example, if you made a post by 10 a.m., and an Instagram user refreshes his news feed around that same time, your post would be the first thing he would see. However, as the day progresses and he keeps refreshing his feed, your post would be ranked lower and lower. It would become buried or ranked below more recent posts made by other users.

One strong factor the algorithm also considers is the subscription level of the user. This simply means the number of accounts the user is currently following. The algorithm monitors the amount of Instagram accounts that a user follows and tries to arrange posts from those accounts in an order of relevance. If a user is following about a hundred different accounts, the algorithm takes note of that and begins to rank each account's content.

You might not know this, but the Instagram algorithm monitors the amount of time that you spend viewing a post. For instance, if a celebrity or top influencer posts a picture or video, and you spend a longer amount of time than usual viewing the post, the algorithm would assume that you are interested in seeing more content like that and begin to rank that kind of content high for your viewing pleasure.

How to Build A Strong Instagram Presence for Your Personal Brand?

Your personal brand needs a strong online presence to thrive and achieve success. Instagram is one of the powerful social media platforms that can greatly boost your personal brand.

So how do you create a strong Instagram presence to help your personal brand?

To boost your Instagram presence, you need to maintain a consistent tone, look, and feel. Let your personal brand be known for something it does. This is to boost brand recognition on Instagram. For example, you could try maintaining a cheery, humorous tone in all your posts and captions.

Also, try as much as possible to interact with your followers. Your audience or followers hold the key to your success on Instagram. Try to reach out to them with your captions. Create an interactive session with your captions and reply to their comments regularly. An example of how you can create an interactive session with your caption is by asking a question. For example, if your personal brand revolves around beauty and skincare, you could post a picture with a caption like:

"Having the right skincare routine is the first step towards maintaining healthy skin. What is your skincare routine like?"

This caption above would encourage your audience and followers to freely engage in the comment section and drop their various skincare routines. To build a strong Instagram presence, you need to strategize your content. Before pushing out your content, plan thoroughly. Instagram is basically a hub for pictures, so you need to constantly post high-quality pictures that tell a story to your audience. Your content should always revolve around your personal brand.

The next step towards building and maintaining a strong Instagram presence is to use the appropriate hashtags. Your hashtags are what boosts your outreach. For example, when you post a picture on Instagram and use the hashtag "#beautytips" or "TGIF," your post would constantly pop up when someone searches for that hashtag. This means that whenever a random Instagram user typed in the hashtag "#beautytips" and searches for it on the platform, your post would be pulled up, depending on how recent it is, and the user can easily click on it.

To build a strong Instagram presence for your personal brand, you need to be active. Keep posting, keep commenting, and keep liking other users' posts. This will help your brand to be noticed easily on Instagram and boost its growth. You can also monitor your progress rate with the use of analytics. The purpose of this is to know how well your brand is doing on Instagram and to find the areas that need improvement.

Tips for Growing Instagram Followers Organically

There are effective methods to grow your following without resorting to buying bot followers. To grow the number of your Instagram followers organically, you need to carry out some research on your target audience. What demographic of Instagram users are you trying to attract? What are their interests? Try to keep the content of your Instagram page aligned with the interests of your target audience. With time, members of your target audience who have come across your posts in there explore page will pick an interest and follow your page.

From Zero to One Million Followers

Don't stop interacting. People are more likely to follow your page if you interact with them on their posts, direct messages, or comment sections. Similarly, when you interact with a related brand that has a large audience, you drive content to your own page. Most Instagram users go through the comment section of brands that they admire. Let's assume that you drop an interesting comment on the post of a similar brand that has about two million active followers. Out of those two million followers, there are about 150,000 casually scrolling through the comments, looking for something interesting. If your comment is catchy enough, they will be compelled to click on your page and follow you.

To improve the level of your Instagram following, you need to cultivate the habit of geotagging in your pictures or videos. Geotagging is simply checking in at a location. Add locations to your posts regularly. Now, what are the benefits of geotagging and how can it help you improve your Instagram following?

Instagram users sometimes search for nearby locations for different reasons. When they click on a certain location, they can see posts with that location added. So, if you added that location to your post in the past, your post will pop up, and the users will be directed to your page.

Giveaways and contests are a foolproof way of boosting your following on Instagram. People love freebies, earning new items or money without putting in much work. To drive traffic to your page you could organize a giveaway. Put up an item or a cash prize and ask your followers to tag their friends to the post. The essence of this is to get your existing followers to convince their friends and followers to follow your page. It's like an ecosystem.

Let's assume that you have one thousand active Instagram followers, and you ask your followers to tag ten friends each to follow your page in order to stand a chance of winning the stipulated prize. Now, if two hundred of your followers participate in that giveaway, they would have tagged two thousand other people.

Eight out of those ten people would follow your page, and you would be boasting about 1,600 new followers. Bear in mind that some of those new followers might also want to participate in the giveaway so you may have up to three thousand new followers, multiplying your initial number of followers four times over. The only thing you must do now is to keep your new followers interested enough so they don't unfollow your page after the giveaway is over. Try to get featured by other Instagram influencers to boost your followers.

How to Use Hashtags Appropriately in Order to Boost Your Instagram Presence and Your Personal Brand.

THE IMPORTANCE OF using relevant and appropriate hashtags has been emphasized. But how do you know the right hashtags to use and how to use them? There are three basic types of hashtags. The first type is the branded hashtag. Branded hashtags are hashtags that you create for the exclusivity and peculiarly of your brand. A branded hashtag revolves around your brand and could be your brand slogan.

- Community hashtags are general hashtags. These are hashtags that have no specific focus and are used by almost every social media user. An example is the popular "#tgif" hashtag.

- Campaign hashtags are hashtags that are created for the specific purpose of creating awareness about a certain issue or event. Most campaign hashtags are short-lived and eventually die down.

The first rule of using hashtags is to create a balance. Popular hashtags will create more engagement, but you don't want to pick a hashtag that is too popular. This is because there is a lot of competition with different results popping up and your own post might get lost under the millions of other posts with the same hashtag. On the other hand, you do not want to use a hashtag that nobody would ever search for on social media.

The best thing to do is to create a balance by using a niche hashtag that would ensure that your post gets the right amount of engagement without choking it with other posts. Narrow down your hashtag. For example, the hashtag "#healthyeating" has about 28.2 million results on Instagram. If your personal brand is based on health and fitness, you may want to avoid using this hashtag as your core hashtag.

This is because you would be competing with 28.2 million people or posts whenever an Instagram user searches for the hashtag.

On the other hand, the hashtag "#healthyeatingideas" has about 69.7 thousand posts. This is a safer and more reasonable hashtag to use. The hashtag "healthyeatingplan" has around 12.7 thousand posts. Reduce your competition but use a relevant hashtag at the same time.

Use enough hashtags on your posts. Instagram allows up to thirty hashtags per post. Utilize this opportunity. The more hashtags you use, the more your post and page appears each time a user searches for a hashtag.

Get creative with your hashtags. You will be amazed at the kind of hashtags that people search for on social media. Don't be left in the dust. The Instagram algorithm is quite easy to beat. Use the right hashtags, boost your engagement and you will be well on your way to having a vast number of followers on Instagram.

Chapter 8:
Facebook to Elevate Your Brand

Facebook is one of the more popular social media platforms that exist. For your personal brand to thrive, you need to be active on a lot of social media platforms. Many arguments have been made concerning the effectiveness of Facebook as a tool for personal branding, and it has been settled that as a personal brand you need Facebook.

Why Should You Have a Facebook Account?

Having a Facebook account is an extra step towards brand development. Your Facebook account helps you to market your brand even more. The Facebook algorithm is friendlier than most other algorithms and guarantees a high percentage of engagement with your audience and followers. If you want to market your personal brand, then you need to have a Facebook account or page.

Facebook connects you with your target audience. One of the tenets of Facebook is to connect people and friends all over the world. Initially, people used Facebook to connect with their real-life friends online. Then, they started using it to make new friends just like any other social network and now, people use it to develop their business and personal brands. It connects you to your potential customers and audience. On Facebook, you can add and follow different users, and you can easily see their line of interests to know if they are the right audience for you.

On Facebook, you can share detailed information about your brand. Facebook is quite straightforward, and if you convey your message correctly, you will see positive results in your personal brand. The basic purpose of Facebook is to connect and share information with people. You need Facebook to constantly share information about your brand to a different user demographic.

Facebook has a very high user demographic. As of early 2018, it had an average of 2.2 billion active users monthly. Sixty-two percent of men and 72 percent of women who are active on social media use Facebook. Why is this important? It is important because your brand will be exposed to a wide array of Facebook users. To get the most out of Facebook, you need to understand the user demographic and build your personal brand around that. You can use the age and gender demographics of Facebook users for the benefit of your personal brand.

Another reason you should have a Facebook account is that it can easily be linked to your other social media accounts such as Instagram and Twitter. This cuts down the amount of work you must do as a brand. For example, if you want to post one picture with the same caption and hashtags on all your social media handles, you can link your accounts, so you only must post once. Hence, if you post a picture on Facebook, it will be duplicated on both your Instagram and Twitter accounts.

How to Get Started on Facebook

THE FIRST STEP TO getting started as a personal brand on Facebook is to define your brand. What is your personal brand about? Carve a niche for yourself and establish it. There are many niches on Facebook, so you must have a clear definition of what your brand is going to be. The purpose of defining your brand is so your target audience has a clear idea of what to expect from you and your personal brand. This would prevent any misunderstanding or vagueness about your brand.

The next step towards getting started on Facebook is to meticulously select who your friends are. Unlike other social media platforms where you cannot select who follows you unless you resort to blocking, Facebook lets you decide who you want to let in your space. This helps in getting rid of internet trolls as you can always unfriend them.

Now, who should be on your Facebook friend list? Your Facebook friend list should consist of other brands with a niche like yours. This will help you to gain more insight and check out your competition at the same time. Your Facebook friend list should also contain your target and immediate audience. Having your audience follow you is not enough. You need to also make sure that you have a huge percentage of them on your friend list as well to create better interaction. You should be very mindful of who you have on your friend list because Facebook has a friend limit of five thousand. You can have as many followers as you want but not as many friends as you want.

After selecting your Facebook friends, you need to devise a strategy for building your personal brand on Facebook. Plan towards increasing your Facebook presence. Your strategy could include mapping out the kind of content to post, how frequently to post, or specific times to post.

Change your privacy settings. As a personal brand, all your Facebook posts need to be public for your followers or people who are not on your Facebook list to see them. Making your posts private would be shutting out your followers, and they would miss out on the experience. It also drastically reduces your engagement on Facebook. For example, let's imagine you have three thousand active followers who are not on your friend list. When you post, about 1200 of those active followers like and comment on your post. If your posts are set to private, those followers will not see it, and then you would lose about 1200 potential likes or comments.

Try to delete unnecessary tags. Certain Facebook just tag you to their posts or pictures for no reason. However, Facebook has a timeline review setting where you can regulate which tagged posts appear on your timeline. If you do not do this, your timeline will be littered with irrelevant posts from many people and will put your audience off.

Tips for Using Facebook To Develop Your Personal Brand

Having established that Facebook can be very beneficial to your personal brand, you need to know the necessary steps to take towards developing your brand with Facebook. As a personal brand, you need to learn the art of networking. Networking here means creating a community of beneficial followers and influencers for your brand. You should try to build relationships with top influencers and Facebook users who can be of help to your personal brand.

Post updates regularly. Your audience wants to keep in touch with you and know what you are doing. Keep making posts for your audience's consumption. If your brand goes out of their sight, it also goes out of their minds. Taking social media sabbaticals would hurt your brand. Daily, new appealing brands are being built, and you must stay on top of your competition. Thus, you should do your best to stay on the radar.

Create a Facebook page for your brand. There is a huge difference between having a Facebook profile and having a Facebook page. While people need to send requests or click on the follow button in order to see posts from your Facebook profile, your Facebook page needs just a 'like' to show the user all your posts. A Facebook page makes your personal brand seem more authentic and professional. Furthermore, a Facebook page would enable you to take more advantage of Facebook ads and sponsored posts. Once your Facebook profile has acquired a huge following, you should create a page to expand your community.

Decide what to write on your Facebook account. Interesting stories or posts will boost your audience engagement and improve your personal brand. Facebook gives you enough room to write as much as you want. Take advantage of this opportunity. Impress your Facebook audience with your writing skills and create amazing content that they can relate to.

Share your story on Facebook. As a personal brand, your audience does not just want to know about your niche or area of expertise. They want to know more about you too. Don't be afraid of sharing your background story with your Facebook audience. This will help you to build trust and grow your personal brand.

Political topics create controversy. Try as much as possible to stay away from politics. This is because your political views or posts may offend a section of your audience who do not agree with them. This could be detrimental to your brand, and you would lose a huge chunk of your following. Focus on creating other relevant content and avoid political talk. Link your Facebook account to your other accounts. This will enable your audience on other platforms to see your Facebook posts and engage.

The Dos and Don'ts of Facebook

For your personal brand to survive on Facebook, you need to take certain actions and avoid missteps. One wrong action can bring your brand crumbling down. Always consider your audience. Your audience is made up of a cross-section of people whose sensibilities vary. As such, you should be very mindful of what you post. A post could offend a section of your audience while the others might not be offended. Posting about vaccines could offend some members of your audience who are against vaccinations. A post about meat would equally offend the vegans in your audience. In the same manner, making offensive jokes would cause you to lose following too. Always try to create a neutral ground and balance.

Do not be mean or insulting towards your audience. People are constantly watching your reactions and personality on social media. Avoid using a condescending tone towards your audience when you are sharing knowledge on a topic. This would make your audience feel insulted, and they would cease to follow your brand.

Put limitations on how much you rant. You should share your story with your audience but don't complain constantly. Nobody likes a complainer. Let's assume you are following a certain user on Facebook. Each day, this user complains about something. He complains about the government. He complains about life. He complains about his neighbors and family. With time, you would get exasperated and tired of his constant nagging tone and cease to follow him. This is the same reaction your audience would have if you constantly nag and rant on Facebook. Try to make uplifting posts for your audience and not posts that will trigger negative emotions.

Do not over share. The goal of having a Facebook account for your personal brand is to share information about your brand. However, do not share sensitive or confidential information. You might have dealings with notable personalities who wish to remain private. Respect their wishes and keep them private. Desist from putting up information like your house address or full details of contracts you have signed in the past.

Use variation in the format of your Facebook posts. Constantly putting up long posts or short posts would make your account seem monotonous and rigid. Vary your format. If you upload a long post today, try creating a short one the next day. If you notice that you have been constantly uploading articles on your Facebook profile or page, change the format by uploading a colorful picture to draw your audience's attention.

Always proofread your posts before uploading them in order to ensure that they are in line with what your personal brand represents. Also, scan your content for errors or contradiction. Although Facebook has an "edit post" feature, it is easier to save yourself the trouble and embarrassment by proofreading thoroughly.

Facebook Ads and How They Work

Facebook ads are adverts created on the Facebook platform that push pages and brands into the news feeds of Facebook users. Facebook ads work by targeting relevant users based on their location, age, gender, interests, and other factors.

To create a Facebook ad, you should know the appropriate audience for your brand. This is your target audience—people whose interests are like what your brand has to offer. How do you find your audience? To find users based on location, select a specific location of your choice. The ad will be shown to users within that location. For example, if you set the location to the United States or an area within the United States, your ad will be shown to Facebook users in the United States or the location which you selected. Facebook ads also work with customer objectives. What are your objectives for wanting to run a Facebook ad? Facebook ad objectives are divided into three broad categories.

- The first category is the awareness category and has two options beneath it. Are you trying to create awareness for your brand, or do you simply want to increase your reach for your Facebook posts? Use the appropriate option and the Facebook ad algorithm will work with it.

- The second category is the consideration category, and you should select this category if you are trying to generate traffic for your Facebook page or profile. Similarly, if your aim is to increase engagement or views, this category is for you.

- The third category is the conversion category. This is basically for situations where you want to increase product sales or get users to register for something. If this category suits your objectives, then a call to action should be included in the Facebook ad.

Facebook ads equally work hand in hand with ad placements. If you want to create an ad for your personal brand, you need to select the places where you want your ad to pop up. Facebook ads can appear either on or off Facebook. Your ad would appear in your Facebook messenger, Instagram, Facebook news feed, and so on, depending on the ad placement you select. To create a Facebook ad, you also need to select the format in which your ad would appear to users. What is an ad format? It is simply the layout of your ad. That is, how it appears on news feeds and other platforms.

Your ad could be in a video format. This means that wherever it pops up, it would show as a video which your target audience can watch. Your ad could also be in a picture format. It would appear as a picture to your target audience. This is the top ad format on Facebook that most brands prefer to use because they feel it retains the audience. However, it is not enough to create Facebook ads. Monitor and measure the effect of the Facebook ad and how it improved your outreach.

Chapter 9:
Reverse Engineering the Facebook Algorithm

The Facebook algorithm is the AI responsible for arranging and sorting Facebook posts as well as creating ads. It tries to make the time you spend on Facebook as meaningful and valuable as possible. Thus, it brings up posts that it feels you would like and interact better with.

How the Facebook Algorithm Works?

The Facebook algorithm underwent a major change in early 2018. It stopped focusing on showing Facebook users posts from business pages and companies and started focusing on showing users personal posts. The algorithm shows you posts from your friends and family first before showing you other posts.

Now, what is the algorithm trying to achieve with this move? The Facebook algorithm wants to improve your Facebook experience by showing you posts that it feels are relevant to you. Its aim is to make every second that you spend on Facebook count. While this move boosts the user experience, it is also a hard hit to brand and business owners.

The Facebook Algorithm focuses on what its terms "meaningful inter-actions," which are basically high engagement. This algorithm gauges the potential interactions a post could generate and ranks it based on its potential. For example, if your post contains relevant factors that would encourage your audience to comment (i.e. important questions, stories, etc.), the algorithm would rank it high on your audience's news feed. It equally tries to predict the posts that users would love to interact with.

This shift in algorithm focus implies that Facebook profiles will begin to be favored over Facebook pages. Business pages may no longer get as much engagement as they once did. Personal accounts with personal content are now deemed to be more relevant to Facebook users than business pages and adverts. Your meaningful interactions on Facebook include the comments on your posts. How many comments did your post generate? The higher your comments are, the higher your posts rank on your audience's news feed. The Facebook algorithm works with a time frame and post recency, but those are not its determining factors. It focuses mainly on meaningful interactions. Therefore, you might see an old post pop up at the top of your news feed because it has a lot of comments. Similarly, a recent post could also rank at the top of your news feed.

Meaningful interactions also include replies to comments and reactions. If your post can garner a high number of reactions from your audience, the ranking increases. If your posts are shared by a high percentage of your Facebook audience, the ranking also increases.

As a personal brand owner, you need to have a firm knowledge of how this algorithm works. It focuses on posts that will create a genuine and authentic connection or interaction among Facebook users. Therefore, your posts containing adverts and engagement baits might not get a high ranking or reach. The algorithm has several ranking factors that determine which posts make it to the top of users' news feeds and the ones that do not.

The Facebook Algorithm Ranking Factors

Ranking factors are the criteria which the algorithm uses to determine the kind of posts that appear on your audience's news feed and the order in which they should appear.

The first ranking factor that the Facebook algorithm considers is the inventory. This has to do with the number of stories and posts available for a Facebook user. The algorithm ranks posts based on the number of available posts. If a Facebook user has about two hundred posts available for him to see, the algorithm ranks those posts in an order. A post's ranking might increase or decrease due to a change in the inventory. For instance, let's assume that there were a hundred and fifty posts and your post was ranked #1 on a user's news feed. Once the slightest inventory change occurs, your post's ranking changes. If a new post appears in the inventory and is better than yours in terms of all the ranking factors, your post would slip down to #2 or even lower.

Another factor that the Facebook algorithm considers is the signals that it gets from a post. The signals it analyzes include the publisher, the post itself, and the engagement on the post.

The algorithm considers the publisher's activeness on Facebook. How frequently does this person make posts on Facebook? If you frequently post on Facebook, your subsequent posts will be ranked high on Facebook. The algorithm also considers the feedback from the person's previous posts. Was it positive or negative? If the feedback from your previous posts is mostly negative, the algorithm would immediately conclude that your recent post is not relevant, and it wouldn't be ranked high. Another signal that the Facebook algorithm watches out for is the type of the post. Is the post a picture, story, or video? Posts that contain important information or are educational are ranked higher by the algorithm. Your post engagement is also crucial to the algorithm. Tags and comments determine how relevant your post will be deemed. For instance, if you upload content and lots of people tag their friends in the comment section, that post will appear frequently on your audience's news feeds. The amount of time a user spends on your post is also a vital signal to Facebook's algorithm. If a user spends a long time viewing your post, it signals to the algorithm that your post is relevant to the user and your post would get higher rankings.

The top third ranking factor is the algorithm's prediction. The algorithm tries to predict your audience's reaction to a given post or content. It tries to gauge the likelihood of your audience reacting and engaging positively on your post and the likelihood of them hiding or disliking a post. This prediction along with the other factors listed above lead to the relevancy score. The relevancy score is how much the algorithm thinks a post would be relevant or interesting to a Facebook user. The algorithm scores each post in the inventory and displays them according to their relevance scores.

Facebook Profiles vs. Pages

Your Facebook profile is different from your Facebook page. A Facebook profile is strictly for your personal use. It contains all your personal information and a community of your close-knit friends and family. On the other hand, a Facebook page is for advertising and posting content related to your brand and business. To create a page, you need to have a Facebook profile first.

Most people who are new to personal branding often wonder which is better for their personal brand. So, let us get down to brass tacks. Which is the better option for your personal brand? A Facebook page or a profile?

Facebook profiles and pages each have their advantages over the other. Both have their peculiarities. For example, if you are trying to grow a larger audience reach organically, you should consider a personal profile. This is because personal profiles have a wide reach. Your Facebook friends and followers can easily see and share your posts, thus creating a wider outreach. The contents of pages do not appear as frequently as profile contents appear. This is a result of the new direction the Facebook algorithm has taken.

On the other hand, Facebook pages are better if you want to sponsor ads and promote content. Personal profiles have no option for paid ads. Only Facebook pages can pay for ads and run those ads on and off Facebook.

Another advantage that Facebook profiles have over pages is that you can have friends and interact with them. Personal profiles are better for building online relationships than Facebook pages. On the other hand, pages are better for measuring your brand's progress. Using analytics, you can measure your impressions, interaction, and engagement on your Facebook page. However, this cannot be done on a personal profile. The issue of professionalism also supports this argument. Most people who have personal brands get confused about the approach to take when trying to boost their brand's professionalism. And so, the argument drags on.

Most of them feel that a Facebook page is more professional than a personal account. To some extent, this is true. A page makes your brand seem official. However, this same effect can easily be achieved on your personal profile. With the right tools, you can make your personal brand look very professional on your profile.

Thus, to boost your personal brand, it is safe to have both a personal profile and a page. Create a Facebook profile first and then gradually extend to having a page. A personal profile helps you to build a large community of friends and audience who will follow your brand, while a page will help you to expand that community and market your brand more.

Facebook Metrics You Need to Monitor

There are certain Facebook metrics that you need to monitor in order to understand how to grow and develop your personal brand. As a growing brand, you should have a firm knowledge of the metrics as they will help your breakdown your progress rate on Facebook.

One such metric is the engagement on your profile and posts. Engagement is the sum of every action that has been taken on your profile and posts. This includes comments, shares, likes and reactions, comment replies, Facebook tags, and so on. You need to monitor your engagement and understand the necessary actions to take towards improving it. Your level of engagement determines how strong your Facebook presence is. Another aspect you should pay close attention to is the number of followers you get weekly either on your profile or your Facebook page. Your friend requests should also be monitored. Do you get more friend requests and followers after making a certain type of post? Do you notice an influx of requests after commenting on posts made by other people? Take note of this to improve your following on Facebook.

You should also take note of your post frequency on Facebook. How frequently do you post? If you do not post occasionally on Facebook, you need to start doing that now. The more you post, the more the Facebook algorithm recognizes you and your personal brand. Think of the Facebook algorithm as a teacher. The more a student answers questions correctly in class, the more the student becomes the teacher's favorite. In the same way, if you make posts frequently, the algorithm will begin to rank you higher due to your activeness on the platform.

Pay special attention to the number of views you get per video. This will help you to see the areas in which your audience's interests lie. Naturally, some videos will get more views than others. Analyze the possible reasons behind your varying video views. Do you get more views when you post a humorous video or when you post a video of yourself? Identify the categories of videos that get more views, likes, and comments for you to be able to post more videos that are relevant to your audience's interests.

Analyze your impressions rate, also. How many times did your Facebook post appear on people's newsfeed?

Finally, the most important metric to consider is your reach. Your reach is the total number of people who can see your post. These people don't necessarily have to be on your friend list or be part of your Facebook followers. They include the number of people who found your posts through sharing by your audience, internal and external links, Facebook tagging, and so on. To develop your brand and get to each member of your target audience, you need to increase your Facebook reach.

How to Increase Your Facebook Reach?

There are certain measures you can take to ensure that your content gets to your target audience on Facebook. Here are a few tips for increasing your Facebook reach. Avoid engagement baits at all costs. Engagement baits are tricky strategies to get more engagement and following on your posts. While engagement baits might be acceptable on some other platforms, Facebook frowns at them, and if you include engagement baits within your content, the Facebook algorithm will automatically reduce the rank of that post. There are five types of engagement baits on Facebook: React baiting, share baiting, tag baiting, vote baiting, and comment baiting. React baiting involves persuading Facebook users to use a certain reaction on your posts. For example, a post saying:

"Use the love reaction if you pour in your milk before cereal and use the ha-ha reaction if you pour in your cereal first".

This post would immediately be flagged as react baiting, and the algorithm will try to hide it from most Facebook users as a penalty. Share baiting is simply trying to manipulate your audience into sharing your posts by posting a photo or content and using a caption like: "Share if you have a relationship like this!" Tag baiting encourages your audience to tag their friends to your post to boost your engagement. For example:

"Tag someone you would like to dance in the rain with!"

Comment baiting is another tricky way of trying to boost your engagement levels. Here, you upload a post and try to get your audience to comment by direct persuasion. Pictures with captions like: " Comment if you have been bitten by a dog before" have elements of comment baiting in them and as such should be avoided.

Vote baiting occurs when you try to get your followers to vote on something, using Facebook reactions. The Facebook algorithm sees this as a ploy to garner more reactions. For example, putting up a post with different options and asking your followers to vote for their choice with specific reactions.

Using engagement baits is one of the fastest ways to reduce your audience reach on Facebook. So, if you want to get a higher Facebook reach, then stay away from engagement baits. Another way to increase your Facebook reach is by utilizing sponsored ads. Facebook gives you the opportunity to advertise your brand for a specific fee.

From Zero to One Million Followers

This ad would appear on the news feeds of different Facebook users depending on the user demographic which you have selected. Facebook ads help to increase your audience reach by displaying your ad both on and off Facebook. To increase your audience, reach, you also need to post quality content. This will encourage your friends and followers to put you on "See First," ensuring that they do not miss any of your posts. With these few tips, you can easily increase your reach on Facebook and popularize your personal brand in no time.

Chapter 10:
The Final Piece: Twitter

Twitter is a massive social media platform that has up to three hundred million active followers. Personal branding entails selling your brand on relevant social media networks in order to draw your audience from every nook and cranny of the web. Twitter can help connect you to your target audience and improve your personal branding. If you own a personal brand, then you need to be on Twitter. This social media platform offers a network of influencers that you could rub minds with. Twitter helps you to stay connected and get more knowledge in areas related to your niche. This social media network gives your brand more visibility. With the sheer number of users that this platform possesses, your brand is given a wider reach of audience to showcase its values and ideas to. Being on Twitter equally makes your brand seem original and more professional.

So, how do you get started on Twitter?

Beginning your personal brand journey on Twitter is quite easy. All you need are a few tips to make your personal brand look professional and impressionable on this social media platform. Getting started on Twitter involves laying the foundation for your brand. The first thing you should do is to pick out a good handle for your brand. Your twitter handle is your username on Twitter. It is the name by which your audience and other brands will identify you and your brand. Thus, you need it to be perfect. Your Twitter handle should be catchy and at the same time, professional. Do not use a name that is irrelevant to your personal brand.

Avoid including numbers and unnecessary characters in your username. This will make you difficult to find on Twitter and make your personal brand seem unprofessional or fake. Your Twitter handle can be coined out of your brand name, your personal name or your initials.

Your Twitter bio also matters. Your Twitter bio is an introduction to your audience. In your Twitter bio, you are introducing yourself and your brand to the audience. Your bio tells people what your brand represents. Thus, your bio needs to be explicit and charming. It should also speak to your target audience. Twitter allows only 160 characters for your bio. So, you must introduce yourself and your brand in less than 160 words. The key to having the perfect Twitter bio is to be creative and straight to the point. Select the main points of your personal brand and express them in as little words as possible. Verbosity has no place in your Twitter bio. Use relevant keywords to make it easier for your target audience to locate you on Twitter. If you have a website, include the link to your website in your bio. This will enable your audience and followers to get more information about your personal brand.

Use a good profile picture of yourself or anything related to your brand. Your profile picture should paint you as being approachable and friendly. To achieve this, use a smiling picture of yourself. Do not upload dark, low-quality images. This will immediately make your personal brand look substandard. Your profile picture is another way through which your audience and other Twitter users can identify your brand. Endeavor to choose the right one.

The next step to go through on Twitter is to pick out the handles to follow. You need to follow users relevant to your brand. The people you follow on Instagram should be within your areas of interest and your niche. For example, you can follow top Twitter influencers or brands like yours. You can also follow users who fall within your target audience. Do not follow random users who would be of no online benefit to you or your brand. The guidelines for people you should follow on Twitter can be summed up in these three questions:

- Are they within your area of interest?

- Are they of any benefit to your brand?

- Are they part of your target audience?

The final step is to link your Twitter account to your other social media platforms. This will make your job of creating and posting content less difficult. After carefully following these steps, you should be ready to use Twitter to improve your personal brand.

How to Improve Your Personal Brand on Twitter

In branding, there is always room for improvement. No matter how good you feel your personal brand is, or how large an audience you command, you can always tweak a few aspects of your personal branding to improve your audience and reach.

Having established this, how can you improve your personal brand on Twitter?

Improving your personal brand on Twitter is quite achievable. One step you should take is to hang on to popular hashtags and tweets. Hashtags signify the topics that most Twitter users are talking about. Twitter popularity is like a train. Hence, you need to jump on this train to put your personal brand out there. Include popular hashtags in your tweets.

The purpose of hashtagging is to create visibility for your handle and brand. When you include hashtags, you are adding your handle to the community of handles that will pop up when a user searches for that hashtag. Hence, you are enhancing brand visibility and exposure. It is advisable to use popular hashtags, but they should not be too popular. One common misconception that people have about hashtagging is the thought that the more popular your hashtag is, the more audience reach you would have. This is not true. Hashtag popularity does not equal audience reach. Your hashtags should be short and unique. Hashtags that are too long will end up eating into the 280 characters limit that Twitter allots per tweet.

To improve your personal brand, you also need to join important discussions that are relevant to your niche. You should know that your target audience's interests are within your niche. Talking or expounding on relevant topics is a great way to connect your target audience with your brand.

For example, if your niche is in the beauty or makeup industry, and a trending topic on Twitter is makeup hacks, you should share your opinion on that topic with your audience. You can share your everyday makeup tricks and include the relevant hashtags. Whenever a topic is trending on Twitter or any other social network, users search for content related to that topic. Thus, you should tap into trending topics in order to reach more members of your target audience.

If your goals include improving your personal brand on Twitter, you need to be ready to adapt. Change and improve the details on your Twitter profile. The only thing that should be left untouched is your brand statement.

Occasionally, change your Twitter bio to provide a refreshing experience for your users. However, your new bio should retain the same message that your former bio conveyed, albeit in different words. Retain the message but change the format.

It should be noted that there is no way to use Twitter. You can constantly tweak it to suit your needs and interests. All you must do is to study the necessary tools that will guarantee your success on Twitter.

The Dos and Don'ts of Twitter

If you want to have a successful personal brand on Twitter and garner an audience who loves you, you need to follow some basic guidelines. Some of the actions you take unconsciously on Twitter could send negative signals to your audience and other users who have come across your profile.

Creating and posting content regularly is an amazing ability but do not limit your actions on Twitter to simply posting tweets. Sometimes, you need to retweet posts made by other brands or users. Retweeting shows your audience your likes and interests. When you retweet a post, you are indirectly telling your audience:

"I endorse this. You should see this too."

Retweeting is Twitter's method of sharing information and tweets. It could also be a way to show support to the brand whose post you just retweeted. When you retweet a post on Twitter endeavor to leave a comment. This conveys to your audience your thoughts about the post and adds additional information.

When tweeting or uploading content on Twitter, try to stay within the character limit. Initially, the character limit was 140 characters per tweet. However, in 2017, it was doubled to a 280-character limit. The trick to using Twitter is to say as much as you can in 280 characters. Your tweets should always be straight to the point.

Avoid creating content that surpasses the 280-character limit or your posts will cut off abruptly. However, if you feel the character limit is too small to effectively convey your message, then you can start a Twitter thread. There is no limit to the number of tweets you can add to a thread. Nevertheless, you do not want to create an excessively long thread as you would lose most of your audience along the line.

Avoid the excessive use of hashtags. When you create a tweet, the maximum number of hashtags contained in that single tweet should be four. When you use too many, the number of words you can write in a tweet is drastically reduced. Thus, you will end up conveying no message at all to your audience and creating a hashtag nightmare.

Do not constantly capitalize. When you post a tweet written all in capital letters, it seems as though you are screaming at your audience. By adding exclamation points to the mix, you will have succeeded in creating a tweet that will make your audience cringe and scroll past.

Capitalizing your tweets can cause your message to be lost. This is because your audience won't focus on the message of your tweet. They will be so distracted by your screen yelling the message will fly right over their heads.

Resist the urge to constantly self-promoter. Talking about your brand all the time will cause you to become monotonous, and your audience will begin to drop off. Let's assume you went on a date with a stranger who would just not stop talking about himself or herself. That is how you look to your audience when you constantly self-promote without a break. Create a balance between your self-promotion posts and your other content. Vary your Twitter content in order not to bore your followers.

As a matter of fact, there are several mistakes that most start-up brands commit when they first get started on Twitter. One such mistake is begging for followers. As a personal brand, you need to grow your Twitter following but begging for followers is not the right way to go about it. There are ways to grow your Twitter following organically. Avoid going to the comment sections and posting comments like:

"Please, follow me" or "Please, follow my profile." This could cause your audience to lose whatever respect they have for your brand.

Also, there is such a thing as tweeting too much. Do not post too many tweets in one day. The maximum number of tweets to make per day should be between six to eight. Excessive tweeting could irritate your audience.

Do not repeat tweets. Sometimes, you might not get enough engagement on a tweet, and you feel tempted to repeat that tweet just in case your audience did not see it before. Don't give in to that temptation. There is every possibility that a certain percentage of your audience saw the tweet but did not find it interesting enough to actively engage. Therefore, you should constantly run a critique of your brand and content.

Always respond to mentions. A Twitter mention is when a user tags your handle in a comment or a post. This could happen occasionally. A follower could mention you in his/her comments or tweet. Never ignore it. Replying to mentions shows your audience that you acknowledge them and are always willing to interact with them.

Avoid dropping on and off the radar. Some personal brands make the rookie mistake of disappearing from Twitter and leaving their accounts dormant in the hopes that they will find it the same when they become active again. This is a huge misconception. When you are dormant, your audience will notice and unfollow you. If you abandon your Twitter account for a month, there is a probability of you losing about 20 percent of your following by the time you return. Don't retweet your own tweets. Imagine this scenario:

You make a joke in a room full of people. Nobody laughs. However, you laugh so hard, you start wheezing.

That is exactly how retweeting your own tweets is like. It is awkward and changes the way your audience sees you. Your job is to tweet and improve engagement. Retweeting your posts should be left to your audience. Twitter is a carefree platform. As such, you should effuse warmth and friendliness on the platform. Do not sound too rigid and uptight or your audience will feel they are dealing with a robot.

What Are the Advantages of Using Twitter for Your Personal Brand?

As a social network, Twitter has many benefits for personal branding. Twitter gives your content a personal touch. Tweets give your audience the impression that your brand is being handled by a human. To retain your target audience, you need to maintain direct dealings with them on all social media platforms. Twitter effectively connects you with your audience and builds a strong relationship with them. Tweeting, retweeting, and live chats all serve to create personal relations between your brand and your audience.

Secondly, Twitter helps you to keep up with the latest social media trends. Staying up to date on trends will help you to adapt your personal brand when it's necessary to do so. Twitter is a veritable source where you can get the trending and viral social media topics. These topics can help you to develop content for your personal brand. Being aware of the recent topics will enable you to join important conversations and improve your brand visibility.

To get the most out of Twitter, you need to devise smart, effective strategies. First, set your Twitter goals. Your Twitter goals are the things you plan to achieve on Twitter within a stipulated amount of time. Twitter goals could include increasing your follower base, improving engagement, and so on. Draw up an outline for the strategies you will need to fulfill the set goals. In the next chapter, we'll discuss the strategies for improving engagement and building a strong Twitter presence.

Chapter 11:
Twitter Algorithm for Massive Engagement

The Twitter algorithm works just like any other social network algorithm. It is interested in improving the Twitter experience for all its users. Now, how does this algorithm work? Twitter has three major sections for tweets. The first section is "Top tweets." This is where tweets which have been ranked high by the algorithm are placed. They are what the algorithm sees as the best tweets for you. The next section of Tweets is the "In case you missed it" section. In this section, the algorithm displays all the trending tweets that it thinks you would love to see or that are relevant to you.

The third section is the section for the latest tweets. Here, the algorithm displays tweets based on their recency. These tweets are arranged in reverse-chronological order. The more recent tweets are displayed on top while older tweets are displayed below.

Your focus should be on the top tweets. What criteria does the algorithm consider when it scores tweets? The first thing the algorithm considers is the interest of your audience. Based on previous interactions, the Twitter algorithm can correctly predict the tweets your audience will be interested in and the tweets they won't want to see. It monitors each user's preferences to find the tweets to display to them. For example, if it notices that a user prefers to look at tweets related to art and photography, it shows those to the user. If your tweets do not fall within the interest areas of your target audience, Twitter may not show it to them.

The Twitter algorithm also considers the past interactions a user has with other Twitter accounts and tweets. Interaction includes liking, commenting on, and retweeting tweets. If a user interacts with another Twitter user very frequently, the algorithm begins to show them more tweets from that part person. For example, if you have been interacting frequently with User A on Twitter, Twitter begins to show you more tweets from User A. Similarly, if your previous posts had a lot of engagement, the algorithm would display more of your tweets. The purpose of this is to ensure that only tweets relevant to Twitter users are displayed.

This brings us to the third factor which the algorithm considers before displaying top tweets: Engagement. Engagement has to do with the number of times your audience clicked "like" on your tweets, commented on them, or retweeted them. It is the visibility ranking of your tweets and profile. The Twitter algorithm takes engagement very seriously, and this is one of the most important criteria you must fulfill if you want your tweets to in the top tweets. When a single tweet has a lot of engagement, the algorithm will conclude that a lot of other users will not want to miss it. Hence, it goes into the top tweets or trending category.

Another important ranking factor is the media. Tweets that contain interesting or appealing pictures, videos, or GIFs get a higher ranking than the ones that don't. This is because videos and pictures typically encourage more engagement. The concept of visual enhancement is more likely to motivate your followers to interact on your tweet.

The algorithm also considers how frequently a user post Tweets. The more active you are, the more the algorithm pushes your content to the top. If you have been dormant for a while and you make a recent post, it would be difficult for that post to have a wide reach.

How to Beat the Algorithm and Create Tweets with High Engagement?

Social media engagement is what every personal brand should strive for. It serves as an indication that you are getting to your target audience and that your brand's reach is increasing. So, how do you create tweets that will give you the massive engagement that you want?

The first step is to build a strong Twitter presence. One thing the algorithm looks at is the Twitter user who is creating those tweets. How strong is his or her online presence? As a matter of fact, the algorithm is not the only one trying to gauge your online presence. Your audience and other Twitter users are doing the same. People are more compelled to engage on tweets if the person who posted that tweet has a strong online presence. Therefore, a celebrity may post a short tweet like: "Good night" and will have a lot of engagement from fans under that tweet. However, when you post that same tweet, you would get no comments or even retweets. If you're lucky, you may get one like from one of your followers.

Another way to get massive engagement is to tweet at the right time. The average lifespan of a tweet is between eighteen to twenty-four minutes. After this time has elapsed, your tweet might get lost under thousands of other tweets. You need to use this lifespan as fast as you can. Tweet during Twitter's peak hours. Most Twitter users are usually online and active between 11 a.m. and 4 p.m. These are the peak hours and you need to create and post your tweets within this time frame. Also, if your tweet is about a trending topic, endeavor to tweet while people are still talking about that topic. This would make it more likely for people to engage. Tweeting about a trending topic after it has died down will get you little engagement because your audience's interest in the topic would have waned. For example, if the trending topic on Twitter is "#UsaElections," you must post relevant tweets while the topic is still trending. If you tweet when it's too late you will get no engagement.

To increase engagement on your tweets, you need to include pictures, videos, or GIFs. These media have a higher chance of getting your audience engaged than your ordinary tweets. For example, let's imagine that you are a student and you see a tweet from a Twitter user that says:

"School is so hard."

You can relate to that tweet, but you would not necessarily feel motivated to like, comment on or retweet the post. Now, imagine if the user had tweeted a funny picture of a student drowning in mountains of books and captioned it:

"Every student's life right now."

This puts a visual effect on the tweet. You would be more compelled to laugh, like, and drop a comment on it. To increase your tweet's engagement, you can promote your tweets on Twitter. This will cost you some money, but it is an effective method of improving your tweet's engagement. The essence of promoting your tweets is to reach a wider number of users. When you promote your tweets, they appear at the top of your followers' news feed. Try as much as possible to reduce the amount of self-promotional tweets. Self-promotional posts will get you little or no engagement. This is because your audience will not be interested in constantly seeing tweets about yourself.

How to Build A Strong Twitter Presence?

Having a strong Twitter presence is important for your personal brand. It improves your brand and tweet engagement. How do you build a strong Twitter presence?

The first step to building a strong Twitter presence is to be active. When you are constantly active on Twitter, you will continue producing quality content to keep your audience hooked and get new followers. Inactive Twitter accounts lose their followers as fast as lightning. Being active on Twitter will help you to realize the right times to post to get engagement. In the same way, activeness on Twitter will get users interested in your brand and put your brand on the map. It also helps the algorithm to prioritize your tweets and boost your reach.

On Twitter, you can become successful by association. To achieve this, you need to follow the right people. Twitter boasts of many influencers and personal brands. To improve your Twitter presence, associate with people who already have a strong Twitter presence, focusing on building networks and relationships with them.

The best way to build relationships on Twitter is by constantly retweeting other users' posts. Retweeting another user's post is a way of endorsing and supporting the Twitter user. When you retweet a tweet, you encourage the user to retweet yours in turn. Thus, you would have built a retweeting relationship.

Make use of Twitter analytics to monitor your engagement, impressions, and promotions to enhance your Twitter presence further. In addition, you can also boost your Twitter presence by creating value and using hashtags appropriately. Creating valuable content will improve brand loyalty. In the same vein, using hashtags would improve your reach and draw more followers to your brand and profile.

How to Use Hashtags Appropriately?

Hashtags have certain unwritten rules guiding their use. Using hashtags, the wrong way can invalidate your hashtag and trump the point of hashtagging. How then can you use hashtags in the right way?

Before using a hashtag, you should ensure that you completely understand the hashtag. Misunderstanding a hashtag could result in a social media scandal or controversy. For example, let's assume that a hashtag meant to campaign against sexual abuse is trending, and you misconstrue it and use the hashtag inappropriately; you could get a lot of backlashes. This could affect your personal brand negatively and you may never recover from it.

Don't use unrelated hashtags. Make sure that your hashtag is related to your tweet. Using unrelated hashtags would make you seem extremely desperate to be noticed, and your audience would be put off. For instance, if your tweet is about reading books or school, avoid using hashtags like #food #makeup or #makeuptricks. This would make you seem ignorant or unprofessional.

Do not space your hashtags. When you want to create a hashtag with two or more words, it is not necessary to use a space to separate the words. Inserting a space would break up the hashtag, and only the word closest to the hash sign would be hashtagged. For example, if you want to create the hashtag, #ThankGodItsFriday, don't space the four words. Inserting spaces will cause only the word "Thank" to be hashtagged and leave the other words bare. Thus, you would have something like this: #Thank God Its Friday.

Similarly, resist the urge to punctuate your hashtags. Inserting a punctuation mark within the hashtag will cause the same effect as spacing. Using the same example above, a punctuation mark would completely ruin the hashtag. If you insert an apostrophe in the hashtag like this: #ThankGodIt'sFriday, the hashtag would break up, and only the letters before the punctuation mark would be hashtagged. Thus, your hashtag would look like this: #ThankGodIt'sFriday.

What makes a hashtag a hashtag is the hash sign (#)? When you create a hashtag without including the appropriate symbol, you are merely creating words, not a hashtag. Always ensure that you insert the hash sign, or your hashtag will be ruined.

Your hashtags should be short. Overly long hashtags would be hard to find when users are searching for hashtags. No user wants to type a hashtag that has about thirty characters. So, if you want your hashtag to be effective, you need to keep it short. Don't use hashtags like this:

#ThankGodItsFridayBecauseIWantToGetDrunkAndEat. That is no longer a hashtag. It has become a sentence. No user would type in a hashtag like that. Also, long hashtags are difficult to remember. Your hashtags should be short to be memorable.

Do not make up your Tweet with just hashtags. This is overusing hashtags. Flooding one tweet with lots of hashtags would only make the tweet seem tacky and unprofessional. Also, you wouldn't have enough characters to send your message. Stick to a maximum of four hashtags per tweet. Hashtagging is one of the fastest ways to boost your reach on Twitter.

Twitter Account Verification

The Twitter platform, just like Facebook and Instagram, has the verification feature. Verified accounts on Twitter are personal or business profiles that have been marked by Twitter as authentic and of public interest. This verification is indicated by a blue badge beside the person's username. Initially, the Twitter algorithm simply monitored profiles and then verified accounts that were of public interest and relevance. However, these days, you can apply to have your Twitter account verified. All you must do is to fill in the verification form with your personal information and submit. If you are qualified to have a verified account, Twitter will verify your account. For your account to be verified, the Twitter algorithm must make sure that your account is not a fake or spam account. Thus, your profile image must be your personal picture, and your account must have been active for up to a year. You also need to have garnered enough public interest and relevance in any niche. Your Twitter account being verified is a stamp of approval from Twitter itself.

Having a verified Twitter account can be very beneficial to your personal brand, making it authentic.

Thus, it places a stamp of authenticity on your brand for the Twitter audience to see. Your brand becomes certified in the eyes of the Twitter community. This would make your target audience trust in you and your personal brand.

A verified Twitter account also builds your reputation on Twitter. It could be a sort of bragging rights that you have earned. It is akin to finally paying off your mortgage or student loans. When Twitter users come across your profile and see the verification badge, it cultivates a bit of respect for your brand. Having your account verified on Twitter will make it easier for you to connect and build relationships with influencers. This is because top Twitter influencers are more likely to want to associate with you and your personal brand if you have a verified account. Thus, if your account is verified, it becomes easier to run in the same circles with them.

Twitter account verification also boosts the security of your profile. Verified accounts are less likely to be hacked into than normal accounts. When you apply for Twitter verification, you fill in your email address, phone number, and other personal information. If your verification request is confirmed and your account becomes verified, the two-factor authentication becomes enabled. Two-factor authentication is a security measure that requires more than one proof of identity in order to access an account.

A verified Twitter account could also bring an influx of new followers to you. People love associating with success, and the hallmark of success on Twitter is a verified account. Also, once your Twitter account is verified, it becomes easier for you to get verified on other platforms. Getting verified on Twitter is morale boosting, and it would widen your audience reach.

However, it should be noted that a verified Twitter account is not set in stone. You can lose your verification if you go against Twitter's rules and community standards. Grievous flouting of the rules can strip you of your verification in an instant. To maintain your verification, follow the rules and keep garnering relevance on Twitter.

It is safe to say that a verified Twitter account is a reward for having built and maintained a strong presence for your personal brand. Once you have a strong Twitter presence and a verified account, you will have achieved a lot for your brand, and you will see the results in your audience reach and engagement.

Chapter 12:
Why Personal Brand is The Key to Success

Personal branding is a way of telling the world your story. It has to do with perception, image, and packaging. The main tenets to follow when building your personal brand is to be yourself. Your personal brand is about you, and you need to be as authentic as possible. The importance of having a personal brand cannot be overemphasized. Anyone can have a personal brand. However, as an entrepreneur or someone with high career goals, you need a personal brand more than most people do. Thus, in this chapter, you will learn how to build your personal brand, and why it is so important to have one.

How to Build A Personal Brand and Be an Influencer?

To create a personal brand, there are certain steps to take. The first step is to lay the foundation of your personal brand. A personal brand without a foundation is like building a house without laying any foundation. With time, it would crumble to the ground. Your personal brand should be based on something. Your personal brand should be based on who you are and what you can do as a person. Your personal brand should be based on your beliefs, skills, passion, value, and personality.

- What do you stand for?
- What are you most passionate about?
- What can you do?

Build your personal brand upon these crucial questions. The next step is to select who your target audience should be. The criteria for selecting your target audience should be based on your interests. If your personal brand is based on software development, then your target audience should be companies and organizations that will be interested in those services. Selecting your target audience can be very dicey. To choose the right audience for your brand, you need to understand the demographic.

- What percentage of people need these services?

- What percentage of people are interested in your niche?

- Which gender makes up most of the demographic?

- What age group are you targeting?

Once you understand this concept, you can go ahead to select your target audience for your brand. You should then strategize and lay out plans. How do you showcase your specialty to your target audience? This is where social media platforms come in. They are tools and platforms through which you can display your brand to your target audience online. You could use Facebook, Twitter, Instagram or

YouTube as your core platform for personal branding. You could also start a blog or a vlog. After selecting your choice medium or platform for branding, you need to map out a plan for developing content. Brainstorm and think of ideas. Create a schedule for developing and uploading content on your social media platforms.

In addition, you could create a personal website of your own. A personal website adds more touch to your identity. It is a way of creating a special space for your personal brand. Your website should display everything your personal brand is about. You could also upload informative content there. Whatever content you upload on your website should be useful and educative to your target audience. Endeavor to share as much knowledge as you can. Don't leave your website dormant. When you leave your site dormant, your target audience will not find it useful. Hence, you should constantly upload useful content.

The Principles of Personal Branding

To get the most out of your personal brand, you need to follow the core principles guiding personal branding. Personal branding is not an easy journey and as such, it has principles to ease the process for new brands. Don't be mediocre or generic. With a plethora of personal brands competing out there, you have no room for mediocrity. If your personal brand reeks of mediocrity, it will be pushed to the bottom of the brand chain. Your personal brand should always be unique in the services it offers, and in the content, it dishes out. The first impression your audience will have about your personal brand is from your social media profiles. A substandard content or profile would kill your personal brand before it has even started.

Always create room for improvement. No matter how amazing you think your personal brand is, you can always improve in one aspect or the other. Run daily critiques on your brand. Try to analyze it through the eyes of a third party. As a personal brand owner, you should never stop learning and gaining new insight. Learn and apply whatever knowledge you gain to your brand.

Your main concern should be your audience. Your audience is the backbone of your brand. They are the factor that could either make your brand a success or taint it. As such, your target and immediate audience should guide your every move and strategy. For example, if you want to carry out a new action with your brand, you should ask yourself:

- How does this affect my audience?

- Would it hurt my following?

When developing any content, you should also ensure that it doesn't negatively affect your audience. It should also revolve around your niche and audience interest.

Adapt and change your methods but never change your niche. Social media and the internet are constantly evolving. This makes it necessary for brands to continuously adapt to suit the changes and tweaks in the system. For example, each time a new social media platform is created, you must adapt and tweak your brand to suit and thrive on that social media platform. Thus, you are constantly changing your strategies and making your personal brand adapt to those changes. However, your niche should be left untouched. Changing your niche disrupts your entire brand and changes the focus. Your niche is what your brand is formed from. Any change in your niche would require you to change and rebuild your audience all over again.

Be creative. Creativity is the bedrock of personal branding. It is what distinguishes you and sets you apart from other existing brands. Think, and let your creative juices flow before taking any action for your personal brand. Creativity is what determines the quality of your content as a brand. The more creative you are, the higher the quality of your content will be.

Your image also matters a lot. Don't do anything that will jeopardize your image and that of your brand. Getting involved in social media scandals or controversies will change your audience's perception of you. You want your brand to trend, but it should not trend for the wrong reasons.

Why Do You Need A Personal Brand?
A personal brand can take you a few steps further in life where your business or career can't take you. Your business and career can be

likened to a bus waiting to take you to your destination. Your personal brand is what fuels that bus and makes it move.

Your personal brand helps you to control your image. In entrepreneurship and business, image and perception are everything. With personal branding, you can control how people see you and your niche. A personal brand is simply you are telling your audience:

- "This is who I am. This is what I do. This is how you should see me."

- Thus, you should have a good personal brand in order to do this.

A personal brand gives you the platform to showcase your specialty and knowledge. One of the purposes of developing a personal brand is to show the world your passion and niche.

A personal brand is an official stamp. When you have skills without utilizing them, you are simply a talented individual. However, developing those skills and morphing them into a foundation for your personal brand turns you into an expert. People will recognize you as an expert in your niche.

For example, let's assume that Miss J is a caterer and she decide to develop her personal brand online. She builds a strong following on any of the social media platforms and starts churning out content and tutorials related to baking. She will become recognized as a baking expert and will get more clients than she did before. A personal brand will also enable you to be remembered for something memorable.

How Does Personal Branding Aid Success?

Personal branding requires hard work, determination, and creativity. All these are requirements for success. When you have a strong personal brand, you are well on your way to success. Personal branding prepares you for success. It teaches you the necessary skills and insight that you need to be successful. Without a personal brand, your journey to success would be long and torturous. You may even lose motivation along the way.

Personal branding aids success through the plethora of opportunities that it offers. When you have a strong personal brand, you are guaranteed to meet people and create connections that will help you on your path to success. As an individual with a personal brand, you will get to go to places you never thought about before and attend important conferences where you can learn, unlearn, and relearn. You will also build important relationships that will grant you success in life. Most successful entrepreneurs today, started out as personal brands. In no time at all, they utilized the opportunities that their personal brands granted them and began to climb the ladder of success. With personal branding, you will gain a lot of insight into areas like entrepreneurship and self-development. To be successful, you must achieve self-development. What better way to achieve this except from personal branding? If you are already a business owner, your personal brand could boost your business by attracting clients. As stated at the beginning of this book, people will be more likely to patronize your business if there is a trusted personal brand connected to it.

Even if you do not want to be an entrepreneur, your personal brand can greatly boost your career. The strength of your personal brand will send a direct message to your potential employers about the value you can bring to their organization. Most companies and organizations seeking to employ individuals would rather pick someone who has a strong personal brand.

Imagine you were an employer and you had to pick between two candidates. In terms of qualifications, they are both equally qualified. However, candidate A has no knowledge of personal branding and no online presence. The last time he posted something online was a couple of years ago. As a matter of fact, when you ran a background check on him, there was nothing negative for you to see. Neither was there anything impressive to find on his profile.

On the other hand, candidate B has managed to build a strong personal brand both online and offline. He has a community of loyal followers and a powerful audience. When you ran a background check on him, you were able to find high quality and informative content that he had developed. You also noticed his strong network of top influencers.

Which candidate would you give the job to? Candidate B! From all indications, Candidate B would add more value to your organization than Candidate A would.

That is the power of personal branding. It completely transforms your resume and makes you look favorable in the eyes of your employer. For entrepreneurs, it pushes you towards the path of success.

Do you have a personal brand? Start developing one today. No matter how unskilled you think you are, a personal brand will bring out your hidden talents. If you are preparing yourself for an amazing position in a company, a personal brand would be of help to your future and career.

1000 Social Media Marketing Tricks

Viral Advertising and Personal Brand Secrets to Grow Your Business with
YouTube, Facebook, Instagram - Become an Influencer with Over One Million Followers

Chapter 1:
Why Social Media Will Transform Your Business

Most businesspersons will agree to the fact that social media is the future of marketing. There is a thick line to be drawn when social media marketing is compared to conventional forms of marketing. More businesses realize that social media marketing is a must-have tool in their marketing strategies. There are many reasons why social media marketing is overtaking other forms of marketing that businesses have been accustomed to. Take, for example, the aspect of cost. With social media marketing, companies get to market their brand at a relatively lower cost compared to traditional forms of marketing. Marketing on social media also aids in boosting your brand recognition among your customers. There are various ways in which social media will transform your business if used appropriately.

Enhancing Brand Recognition

One thing that you must understand about social media is that there are billions of people spending hours daily communicating with friends, relatives, and brands like yours. These are your potential customers. The benefit that social media gifts you are that it brings together the customers that will likely be interested in the products and services you offer. With the help of social media, customers come together to create an online community. How you interact with them will, therefore, make a huge difference to your brand.

Brand awareness is vital to the growth and success of your business. Without a doubt, the more customers know about your product, the more likely you are to sell your brand. Keeping in mind that billions of people interact together on social media, this means that it is a great place to build brand awareness.

Enhancing brand awareness does not happen overnight. The way you use social media will have an impact on the extent of brand recognition that you will have. So, here are some pointers to help you in enhancing your brand recognition among your audience.

Make Good Use of Visual Content
The internet is filled with all sorts of information regarding how to make use of social media networks. However, it is worth stating that not all content is worth digesting. Consumers have grown to learn how to filter out content that they feel is less desirable. Accordingly, it is imperative to understand that the content you post will determine whether people will share it or not.

When posting on social media platforms, it is recommended that you embrace the idea of posting visual content. Why? Visual content is more engaging. Social media users are more likely to share visually appealing images and videos compared to text. Therefore, entice your audience by posting visual content.

Cultivate on Having A Unique Voice

The mere fact that you are interacting on digital platforms does not mean that you will be talking to robots. Communicating on social media means that you will be engaging with human beings—therefore, you should act like one. Your brand personality should be developed naturally. Your posts should reflect the type of brand that you are. Your character will aid you in garnering more followers to your end. For instance, if your brand is perceived as transparent, rest assured that you will have more followers coming your way.

Use Different Tones but Remain Consistent

With the vast array of social media platforms out there, you should understand how to interact in every one of them. The people that you associate with on Facebook are the same people that you will be interacting with on Twitter. The last thing that your audience needs is for you to be boring. Posting similar content all across the different platforms will only make your brand boring. It is essential to understand that there is a reason why social media users have different social media accounts. Some may look for excitement, while others look for information. So, keep in mind that what you post matters most. For example, if you are going to post on LinkedIn, your audience expects you to be professional. On the contrary, your audience on Facebook expects you to be friendly and more casual.

Share Quality Content

Quality content will bring thousands of followers to your side. If your audience finds your content to be interesting, they will be motivated to share it with their friends. Conversely, if your content doesn't arouse interest, rest guaranteed that it will not be shared. The number of shares will be reliant on the type of information you post. Consider your day-to-day social media use; what motivates you to share content? Indeed, you will look for something that captures your attention uniquely. It is the same thing when it comes to posting information about your brand. People should find your content as informative and worth liking or sharing.

Follow Influencers

Who are influencers on social media? Well, simply stated, influencers are those individuals that have the power to influence social media users to follow your brand. Influencers have a large number of followers that trust in their actions on social networks. Therefore, by following them, you could gain the advantage of pulling a large following to your side. Following influencers requires that you listen to what they often talk about. Engaging with influencers brings your brand to the limelight. This is because more people will become aware of your brand existence through the way you interact.

Join Groups

Social media is all about joining the bigger social community over the internet. As a business, you have to be social. Consequently, make a point to enter the groups that are associated with what your brand promises to offer. While joining these groups to interact with your audience, it shouldn't be that obvious that you are there to sell your brand. A more natural form of interaction will leave your brand in the minds of your audience. They will keep pondering about how your brand understands them. So, build a presence that will influence people to follow your brand. Ultimately, this will raise awareness, and your brand will grow.

Know How to Start Conversations

Knowing how to start conversations will make a significant difference in your social media marketing efforts. The best way to start a conversation is by asking questions. Take your time to research on the most exciting topics and pose questions about them. Find engaging topics that will keep your audience debating. It is imperative that you also participate in these debates to ensure that your audience understands what your brand is all about.

Keep Off Politics and Religion

Politics and religion are two sensitive topics in society today. Since your industry is not related to politics or religion, ensure that you avoid discussing. Consumers will find your brand annoying if you take sides. Therefore, get this fact clear to guarantee that you are not despised by the people you expect to depend on your brand.

Gaining Trust from Your Customers

Marketing on social media will also transform your business by increasing its credibility. The more you post quality content on different sites, the more you gain trust from your customers. For example, you could try posting personal experiences from your customers. This gives other followers a reason to believe in your brand. The best part about using social media is that it can also help you in dealing with any negative reputation that your business might have suffered from. Strategic content could assist you in gaining the trust that you once had with your customers.

Increasing Sales

It should be noted that many followers on social media do not guarantee 100% sales returns. This means that many followers do not necessarily see that your brand will be highly rated among your audience. However, the more popular your brand is, the better. It increases the chances of boosting your sales in the long run. Hence, your brand could be transformed with the help of social media marketing through increased sales.

Enhanced Ways to Connect with Your Target Audience

Your business will also benefit using social media as you get to use better strategies to communicate with your target audience. For instance, you could choose to categorize your audience based on their purchasing behaviors, interests, demographics, etc. Consequently, you get to interact with your audience on a more personal level. By focusing on their purchasing behaviors, you could tailor your content to suit their demands. This implies that you will post content that would highly likely entice your audience. As such, social media marketing transforms your business by offering you better ways of connecting with your target audience.

Reputation Management

The remarkable aspect of social media is that its users are always talking about brands in the market. Therefore, whether you are on social media or not, people will keep talking about your business. Whether you choose to join social media groups or not, people will keep talking. This infers that, if you are doing the right thing; socially, you will be better placed to manage your brand's reputation. Businesses are regularly advised to engage in conversation and actively interact with their followers on their social media pages. It helps manage the brand's reputation. For instance, if customers are speaking ill about a specific brand, the business could step up and talk to their audience politely.

Drive Attention to Your Website

Entrepreneurs are also using social media to drive traffic to their sites. From the posts that they make, their target audiences are made aware of the existence of the business websites that they could turn to. Business owners are, therefore, advised to share engaging content that will spark attention in the minds of consumers. When posting, for example, on YouTube, it is wise to focus on a landing page that will drive people to your business website.

With the various ways in which social media could transform your business, it is worth investing in it. It is the "in thing" in marketing today. Numerous companies are using social media as their primary marketing platform. The best part is that most of them have realized that marketing on social media is not only cost-effective, but it also opens doors to a wide array of benefits. Accordingly, it is never too late to create a business social media account and invest in understanding how best to operate it.

Chapter 2:
Understanding Social Media Marketing Process

Marketing on social media is different from the conventional forms of marketing you might be used to. However, this does not mean that marketing on social media is a daunting task. Quite the opposite, marketing on social media requires one to have a good marketing strategy. This will ensure that they get the best out of their marketing efforts. Undoubtedly, marketing on social media is the best way in which a brand can communicate with current and prospective customers. The advantage gained in using social media is that one can conveniently communicate with their target market without spending much money. Moreover, there is also the benefit of the immediate feedback gained.

With the benefits that are associated with using social media as a marketing tool, it is imperative for a business owner to understand the process of marketing on social media. Honestly, millions of business owners are doing it. Sadly, only a few of them benefit. There are those that spend millions on having a social media presence, yet they do not profit. Why does this happen? Well, this happens because they fail to understand the uniqueness of marketing on social media. They fail to comprehend that several factors could make them stand out when marketing on social platforms such as Twitter and Facebook. Some of these factors are succinctly described in the following lines.

Strategy

So, now that you have created your Facebook business page, the next thing you are thinking of is to post content, right? Sorry to disappoint you, but this is the last thing that you ought to be thinking of. Before setting up your social media page, the first thing that you should do is to have a well-documented strategy. The strategy that you adopt will define the goals that you have in mind. Also, your strategy will help you in correctly identifying your target audience, depending on the products and services that you will be offering. Besides, having a clear plan will also help you in knowing how best you can grow your business with time.

Consequently, before thinking of setting up any social media page that your business will use, take your time to draft a strategy. This is an area that will be closely looked at in detail later in this book.

Reasonable Expenditure

One huge mistake that business owners often make is that they consider social media marketing as the best way of marketing their brand for free. There is that perception that marketing on social pages is free. Indeed, it is free. Nevertheless, if you want to get the best from these pages, you will have to invest something. Businesses that have profited while using social media to market their products will attest to this fact. You have to invest both time and money to guarantee that you reap the benefits of using social media to market your products and services. In this case, you will have to incur expenses in paying for ads and find ways of hiring the best team to join you—both require money.

Consistency

A trick to winning over followers on social media is consistency. Posting several things today and failing to post the coming week will certainly not get you the liking that you desire. Your followers expect you to keep posting. You should post on your wall daily as this is what your audience expects from you. Keep in mind that people visit social media pages every second. As such, if possible, it is recommended that you should have a reliable team working to make sure that content is posted regularly and daily.

Value

When browsing through social media posts, what is it that gets you to like a post? Ask yourself this question, and you will know what people expect from you. Your audience is out there hoping to get some form of value from what you post. Don't just post anything simply because you can. Displaying the right content will get people talking about your brand. To know the right content that suits your audience, you will have to do a little research about them. The good news is that there are many tools that will help you in monitoring and understanding your clients. Therefore, you will find it easy to post things that are relevant.

Giving It A Personal Touch

Some businesses approach social media marketing as a company. Unfortunately, they end up failing in their marketing efforts. Some of these companies end up claiming that marketing on social media doesn't work—but it does! With the right strategy, marketing on social media will make your brand famous out there. Your brand could become a household name if you understand how best to utilize social media to your advantage.

Concerning the above, it is vital that you approach social media by giving it a personalized touch. Don't offer your clients the perception that you are in this to make money. First, take your time to win them over. Find the right voice that will make your audience feel appreciated. Get social in a way that you will not scare your target audience. Once they interact with you on a personal level, rest assured that your posts will be shared all over.

Follower Engagement

Most people would post numerous things on social media and expect many followers; this is what most businesses do. It is important to note that the number of followers that you have on social media does not matter if there's no engagement. If your followers on Facebook or Twitter do not interact with your brand, then they are of no use to your business. Therefore, it is wise that you find a way of engaging with your target audience regularly. Keep the conversations going with the groups that like your brand and get them talking about your brand by asking them questions or posting content that requires to be shared. By doing this, you will be giving your audience a reason to have your brand in mind each time they communicate on Facebook, Twitter, LinkedIn, or Instagram.

Calls to Action (CTA)

Having the right calls to action is part of any successful social media marketing strategy. With the right call-to-action message, there is a certainty that your audience will be directed to your business page. When posting on social media, your main goal is to drive your audience to your business page. Alternatively, the primary goal that you have in mind is to drive your customers to purchase a specific product that you are selling. You want them to buy the product that you are advertising on social media. The reason for marketing on social media is to generate revenue for your business. Therefore, you should formulate an excellent CTA where your customers are enticed to purchase a product or to depend on the services that you provide.

From the information provided, marketing on social media is not as difficult as you might have thought. The only thing that you need to understand is that there are certain tricks of ensuring that your marketing efforts pay off. For instance, when engaging in such marketing for the first time, have it in mind that you need to invest your money

Gary Jake

in it. Yes, marketing on the internet might be free. Nevertheless, if you want to counter competition from your rivals, you will have to do a little more. You must invest your money in paying for adverts and building the right team behind you. Equally, you will have to focus on the value that you give to your target audience. They yearn to be associated with a brand of quality. Hence, post content that will get them intrigued and proud of you. All these are but a few pointers on the process of marketing on social media. Stand out from the rest by keeping these factors in mind.

Chapter 3:
Top Social Media Platforms

Now that you have decided to make a considerable leap and invest in social media marketing, it is essential that you know of the pages that you should be investing in. Ideally, with numerous social media pages out there, it is easy to get confused on the best platform that suits your business. The popularity of a social media page should not be the reason for you to choosing it as a means of marketing. Different social media pages work differently. There are those that might not suit your business because your target audience does not use it frequently. So, it makes sense that you take your time in understanding the different platforms that are out there.

Before jumping into detail, let's take time to understand social media in general and how people use it to communicate.

Social networking pages such as Twitter, LinkedIn, Facebook, and Instagram have become famous recently. More people are turning to social media as a way of communicating. Interestingly, most people have more than one social medium account. This means that regardless of the social media page that you invest in, there is a like-lihood that you will get followers to like and share more about your brand.

Besides communicating with friends and relatives, individuals rely on social media to make their purchasing decisions. Gone are the days when folks would rely on word of mouth to purchase a certain prod-uct. Today, people log in to their social media accounts and query about the brands that they are about to turn to. This means that mak-ing purchase decisions have been made easier than ever before. Peo-ple do not need to talk to their friends to understand that a certain brand is good or not. They rely on what people are saying about a specific brand over the internet. So, if people are talking positively about your brand, there is a good chance that you will run a profitable business.

There is also the aspect of recommendation that socialites keep talk-ing about. If a customer is impressed with the products and services that you offer, there is a good chance that they will recommend your brand to their followers. This is what makes social media quite inter-esting: as people grow to love your brand, they try their best to share the good news to their followers on different platforms. This implies that a good brand reputation will get the most out of social media. The referral program will help them a lot as they depend on products and services that have been tried and tested for quality performance.

Finding the right brand to stick to has never been so easy thanks to social media platforms. Unfortunately, there is a risk associated with such convenience that users find in using social media to gain information. If your brand has a bad reputation, it means that the news will also spread like wildfire. So, it is worth investing in building a good image for your brand that will sell it on social media.

Some of the best social media pages that your business should invest in will be briefly discussed in the following paragraphs. Information delivered here will help you in better understanding which social pages are ideal for your business.

YouTube

YouTube stands as one of the best platforms that you could use to market your business. The central reason for this is because of the type of content posted. YouTube has grown in popularity over the past few years due to its visually engaging content. About 85% of adults claim to visit YouTube regularly. With the huge number of people using YouTube to entertain themselves, this presents itself as a good opportunity for businesses.

The number of views that you gain on YouTube could transform your business overnight. The more views you get on your channel, the higher your chances of making profits from your business. Companies are making fortunes from this platform, as all they need to do is to post. Therefore, depending on the videos that you will share, you will pull a large following to your side.

Just like any other platform that you will use to market your brand, there many factors that you have to bear in mind. These factors will make a difference in whether you will get higher rankings or not.

Keywords

To ensure that you benefit from using YouTube as your ideal marketing platform, you should optimize your channel using keywords. Keywords will help search engines such as Google to understand your content. Therefore, optimization will increase your ranking not only on search engines but also on YouTube.

Video Title

Chances are that you know the importance of creating a lasting first impression when you meet with someone for the first time; well, the same thing applies to YouTube. You must create a lasting first impression with your video titles. Users will click to watch a video that has an enticing title. Hence, this is a strategy that you should use to make certain that you attract a large audience to your side. Online marketing experts argue that shorter titles are always the best. This is because longer titles could be cut off depending on the search engines or the browsers that your audience uses. Thus, it is worth keeping in mind to benefit from promoting your brand on YouTube.

Video Description

Besides having a good title for your video, it is also significant to have a good description. Video descriptions aid search engines to determine the type of content that you are posting. This shows that if you fail to provide a solid description, search engines will find it difficult to ascertain the content you are posting. Consequently, expect your rankings to suffer greatly. It is recommended that the video description should be roughly 250 words. While writing your description, keep in mind that keyword use is vital.

Facebook

Facebook is yet another highly ranked social media network that you could use to promote your brand. Over the years, Facebook has maintained its position as one of the leading social networking websites. With over two million monthly active users, you can be confident that your brand message will get to the people that you want. Facebook has taken strides to gain a competitive advantage over rival companies due to the acquisitions that it has made over the past few years. Recently, it took over WhatsApp. Other core products of the company include Facebook Messenger and Instagram.

Just like marketing on YouTube, there are some things that you need to bear in mind when marketing on Facebook.

Hosting Facebook Contests

One of the main tricks that Facebook business users employ in increasing the number of followers is by hosting Facebook contests. It aids in building brand awareness not only to your target audience but to prospective clients. You should understand that these contests cannot be hosted on Facebook. Instead, they are just a way of directing your audience to the physical place where the contests will take place.

You need not to worry about designing the contest ads for yourself. Various paid tools can help you get the job done. There are also tons of free tools that offer free contest templates for you to take advantage of. Ensure that you settle for the best models that will strike your audience attention from the word go.

Quality of Your Ads
Quality ads will influence the perception that your audience has regarding the adverts that you will be posting on Facebook. Without a doubt, an advert that is regarded as informative by your audience will be shared all through. On the contrary, if your audience perceives your adverts as a nuisance, they will ignore it. Some might end up turning off notifications coming from your end. Therefore, you should be careful about the quality of the ads that you post.

The Relevance of Your Ads
Facebook users are keen to ensure that they gain access to contents that matter to them most. This means that if your content is considered irrelevant, it will negatively affect your brand. So, chances are

you are asking yourself about how you could improve the relevance score of your posts. Here are some points to get you started.

Target a Broader Audience

While it is advisable to narrow your target audience, it is also beneficial that you target a more general audience as a way of improving your relevance score. When marketing your brand on Facebook for the first time, it is important to focus on a large customer base. A large customer base will open doors to people that could be interested in the products and services that you offer.

Keep Things Fresh

I believe that you have an active social media account that you currently use. One thing that annoys you is perhaps seeing the same ad constantly; well, your audience feels similarly. They get bored easily with advertisements that constantly repeat. To win your customers over, you should not be the brand that has the same Facebook ad causing a nuisance to customers. If you are targeting a small group of people, this should be a priority. Make sure that you have different advertisements selling your brand with a similar tone. Most importantly, don't forget to add some humor in the ads that you create.

Season

Undeniably, the relevance of your ad will be affected by the season that you choose to post the ad. If you post when demand is low, then your ads might be considered as irrelevant. Before posting any

Facebook ad, ensure that you are posting it at the right time of the year. For example, if it is January, you should post ads about enjoying the holiday in your hotels.

Optimize Your Ads

Your ad relevance will be given a massive boost if you bear in mind that you need to optimize your ads. Who are you selling your products/service to? Are they interested in what you have in store for them? Asking yourself these questions will help you in knowing what your customers expect from you. Also, you will find it easy to customize your ads to match with their demands.

Don't Just Sell Your Brand

Another consideration to keep in mind when promoting your brand on Facebook is the way you communicate with your audience. Selling might be the goal that you need to do, but it should not be that obvious. Find a way of keeping your audience engaged with the content that you post. Remember, posting quality content will influence your followers to like and share your content. Marketing experts recommend that you could keep your audience fascinated by sharing funny videos, posting questions, and other forms of useful content. All these begin by first understanding who your audience is.

Remember to Link Up with the Right Groups

The Facebook groups that you join will make a difference in your marketing campaign. Marketing experts did not forget to mention to you that joining these groups will make it easy for you to find your ideal target audience. Therefore, ensure that you research the best groups that are directly related to what you are offering. Choose groups that are active as this guarantees that you reach out to active Facebook users.

Understand Why People Share

The secret to attracting a large following begins by understanding why people share in the first place. Facebook brings people together as a large community. People share to be informed and entertained. Therefore, before posting any content on Facebook, you should consider whether it is informative and entertaining at the same time.

Realizing the psychology behind sharing of social media content gives you the benefit of knowing how to customize your content. This is because you will be sharing business content that will have a direct impact on your followers.

Instagram

As you browse through the top social media pages that your business could depend on, you will find Instagram as one of the best. Instagram is considered an essential marketing tool due to its huge fan base. With over 500 million active users globally, your business could easily reach out to its clients. Part of Instagram's fame stems from the fact that it is visual. This means that users are more engaged when using Instagram compared to other social media pages. There are several advertising options that you have at your disposal when using this platform. They include:

- Photo adverts

- Video adverts

- Carousel adverts

- Stories adverts

- Collection adverts

There are more than 25 million Instagram business profiles globally. However, this should not discourage you in creating your personalized Instagram page. Businesses create new accounts daily, and they win over clients. Consequently, you should not be left out. There are a few marketing tips that you should consider when using Instagram to build your brand.

Relating to Your Followers

It is imperative that you have the mindset of your followers each time you market your brand on social media. Having this mentality ensures that you personalize your ads to suit your customer demands. Your clients could have varying reasons as to why they are on Instagram. For example, some of them are there to kill time. Others are there to catch up with their friends and relatives. So, it is worth understanding your audience in ways that guarantee you deliver the right message to them.

Don't Over-Post

Over-posting is the last thing that you should be doing on Instagram. Yes, your audience needs to hear from you; but it doesn't mean that you should keep posting and posting. When you do this, you are not selling your brand. Instead, you are yelling at your customers. They don't expect this from a brand that they plan to be loyal to in future. The recommended number of posts in a day is one-to-two posts. Equally, you should understand that there are certain recommended times that you should be posting. Early morning at 8 a.m. – 9 a.m. is highly advisable. Also, you could post at 2 a.m. The reason why you should schedule your posts at the right time is that there are times when people don't have time to go through their feeds. Nevertheless, if you post at the right time, you increase the chances of boosting your reach.

Promote Your Instagram on Other Platforms

Your business Instagram page should be promoted on other social networks that you have. For instance, your Instagram icon should be added to the Facebook or Twitter business page that you use. The importance of connecting your Instagram with other social networks is that it pulls together your friends and other followers. Reminders about your Instagram page should be sent across all the social platforms you are active in. You could also make a point of encouraging your employees to add the business Instagram icon on their email signatures. This is another way in which you promote your Instagram page.

Learn from the Best

Experience is the best teacher. There are those companies that have utilized social media pages to their advantage and are making millions. What are these companies doing that you are doing differently? This is the question that you must have in mind. If possible, you can steal ideas from your rival companies. While doing this, you should be keen as it could raise a red flag among your esteemed customers. Try to get inspiration from social activities that make successful companies stand out from the rest of you in the same industry.

Make Good Use of Instagram Tools

There is a good reason why there are plenty of Instagram tools at your disposal. Some of these tools will help you in making your photos appealing. Other tools will help you gauge how good your brand is performing. Without a doubt, these tools will help you become a good marketer. Some of the Instagram tools that come highly recommended include VSCO, Word Swag, Enlight, Afterlight, and Facetune.

Use Product Teasers

Selling more products on Instagram will require some creativity from your end. Product teasers will be a good tip that will keep your audience wanting. While trying to tease them on the huge discounts that you are offering, you should remember not to be too pushy. What you are after is to increase the excitement that comes with purchasing your product or depending on your service. Perhaps another effective way of teasing your followers is by showcasing images that prove you offer variety. Your followers will be tempted to opt for your products since you have a wide array of options for them to choose.

Twitter

Twitter is another powerful social media marketing tool that you should consider taking advantage of. Numerous brands are successful from only posting on Twitter. However, there is a trick to becoming the best when using Twitter to promote your business. First, you should know that there are over 200 million active Twitter users worldwide. Therefore, this is a great place to market your business. The good news is that the statistics are not stagnating any time soon. The number of Twitter users grows daily. This means that your business stands an excellent chance of developing if this platform is utilized effectively.

So, how do you make the best out of Twitter as a marketing platform?

Make Use of Twitter Cards

If you have used Twitter before, then you are aware of Twitter cards. These cards help in making sure that your tweets stand out. The use of these cards will give a lasting first impression in the minds of your audience; thus, your message will attract a large following.

Twitter Followers

The way you interact with your following will have a significant impact on your brand awareness. Don't just depend on a large audience that is not engaged with your brand. Having a large audience is useless if there's no engagement. Therefore, it is up to you to make sure that your customers continuously talk about your brand. They could be talking about the improvements that you have made or the changes that they expect to see in your brand. Fortunately, several tools can help you in sticking to relevant followers. These tools analyze your audience and determine ideal conversations that you should hold with them.

Engage with Influencers

Influencers are regarded as the only shortcut to getting a large following. These people have a large following behind them. Therefore, their influence on your marketing campaign could be phenomenal if you know how to interact with them. Build a lasting relationship with these influencers, and you will benefit from the followers that would opt to rely on your brand.

Remember to Utilize the Right Hashtags

Communicating on Twitter is different from communicating on other social media platforms. In Twitter, users use "hashtags." Your tweets should incorporate the right hashtags that will generate a higher engagement rate with your followers. Social media marketing gurus recommend that you should shorten your hashtags. Twitter users are more likely to interact with others when your hashtag is short.

Pay Attention to Your Competitors' Actions

Your competitors can help you know the right audience that you should target when communicating on Twitter. You should find out who your adversaries are interacting with. What are they talking about? Which hashtags are they using to communicate? Do your research to understand how you will counter their competition. This is what they are doing, so, you should also do the same to remain competitive in the industry of operation.

Your Headlines Matter Most

With the high number of Twitter users globally, you should be creative enough to attract a considerable following. To achieve this, you need to stand out from the rest. Your headlines will sell your brand in ways that you never expected. The headlines that you use will create a lasting first impression and ultimately ignite some retweets here and there. People will not like your tweets if at all the headlines are just dull. Create catchy phrases that will keep your audience glued and that they would want to know more about your brand.

Chapter 4:
Grow Your Business with YouTube

Businesses that seek to thrive in their market of operation must incorporate smart marketing tactics. Ideally, with the competitive environment that companies operate in today, there is a dire need to be creative. With the advent of the internet, however, marketing over the internet has opened doors for a different kind of competition. Small businesses have found ways of marketing their products without incurring a lot. Their strategies have also changed. More and more companies are switching from marketing on TV to selling their products on the internet.

Today, businesses have realized that YouTube is not only used for personal video sharing, but it can also be used to endorse brands. This is made possible because YouTube has over 1 billion users. Besides, up to 300 hours of video are posted every minute to the platform. That is not all; about five billion videos are accessed by people daily. Therefore, YouTube presents itself as an excellent platform to market your brand.

The best thing about YouTube is that there is no limitation to the type of business that can make use of it as a promotional tool. Whether small or large, your business could exploit the benefits that accrue in using this platform. One of the main reasons why YouTube is an ideal platform to promote your brand is because of the video content that is shared. Videos keep people engaged and are more effective than text. People could spend hours watching videos as they are more entertaining compared to text.

Moreover, videos also encourage people to act. Accordingly, your promotional videos could motivate your audience into making a move and depend on the products and services that you offer. Quality posts on your YouTube channel could direct your viewers to your business home page.

YouTube users also consider this platform as convenient since they can get the information they need easily. Searching for videos on YouTube is pretty easy. With the right keywords, a video could be found in seconds. Similar convenience is gained when searching for videos on Google. Also, related videos usually pop up when one watches a video. Thus, if you are promoting a line of products, similar videos on other products that you are promoting will be listed for a user to gain access to.

Benefits of Using YouTube to Promote Your Brand

Maybe you are still wondering why you should settle for YouTube as your ideal marketing platform. If this is the case, let's consider some of the benefits that you gain when using this platform to promote your brand.

Popularize Your Brand

Are you trying to promote a new brand that hasn't hit the market? Well, YouTube is a great place to start. This is because it offers you a place where you get to showcase how your product functions. The platform also gives you time to explain to your audience the benefits that one can gain by using your product. If your product solves a problem that people are experiencing, there is a high chance that you will get many likes and shares.

Get Feedback

Entering new marketing is always a challenge. You never know what your customers will say about the product or service that you plan to offer them. However, with the help of YouTube, you can evade the whole dilemma. It gives you a place where you can get the feedback that you need even before introducing the product in the market. Take a quality video of the prototype and upload it on YouTube. If you get positive responses, you can go ahead and introduce the product after adjusting per your customers demand. On the contrary, if you get negative reactions, this might be an indication that you are introducing the wrong product to your target market.

Sharing Made Easy

As your business strives to grow, there is the chance that you have a team working for you from remote locations. Therefore, sharing information might be a challenge for you. Relying on YouTube to share presentations with them could help you. Your workers from distant locations will access the video and work to build your brand as you desire.

Streamlining Tasks

We cannot refute the fact that there are times when your product will have problems. Your customers might face challenges when using your product. Mitigating these problems could be a nightmare if you don't know where to start. YouTube can quickly solve this problem. All you need to do is post a video showing how your clients could deal with the challenge they are currently facing. Your video could solve a huge problem that could have required the need to manufacture a different product.

Increase Your Brand Awareness

Communicating on YouTube is quite easy. Businesses create their channels where they post videos relating to their brand. Interestingly, certain businesses don't need to post to get noticed. By making comments on videos that are related to their brands, they increase their brand visibility. However, it is highly recommended that a business should have a personal channel to expand its brand visibility on this platform.

Taking Advantage of YouTube Insights

Besides analyzing your target audience through the comments that they make; a business owner can also rely on analysis tools that are available on YouTube. For example, rating tools will help one in knowing how their brand is performing on this platform. There is also an insight feature incorporated; it aids in getting statistical information regarding the individuals watching your channel. Without a doubt, this is what your business needs. You will know whether the promotional campaign is working to your advantage or not. If things are not working as you expected, you can easily adjust.

Drive Traffic to Your Business Website

Apart from posting videos to your channel, you could also insert relevant links to the videos that you post. This means that you will be driving traffic from YouTube to your business page. For that reason, your target market will quickly find your business as you have promoted it all over YouTube.

You Get to Save Money

Cutting down on your marketing expenses is perhaps one of the main goals of every business. Conventional forms of marketing such as radio and television were quite expensive. Nonetheless, with YouTube, you get to cut down on your marketing costs. One fact that you should bear in mind is that posting videos on YouTube is free. You spend nothing in setting up a channel where your business will establish its online presence. Your marketing strategies will make a difference as to whether you will ultimately reap the benefits of marketing on YouTube or not. So, play your cards right.

You Earn Money
Besides the fact that you will get indirect benefits coming your way, you also get paid by posting relevant content on YouTube. This infers that the more you post, the higher your chances of getting a paycheck. Google AdSense video will determine the amount of traffic that you are driving from your posts, and you will get paid. Consequently, you need to polish your content regularly to ensure that you attract a large following to your business channel.

With the numerous benefits that will come your way when using YouTube to market your brand, you should opt to add it as part of your primary marketing tool.

How to Use YouTube to Endorse Your Brand
Considering the vast array of businesses that depend on YouTube to promote their brands, it goes without saying that there are various ways of using the platform. Your business goal might be different from your rivals' business goals. Therefore, your YouTube use will vary.

Some companies use YouTube to increase their brand awareness, while others use it to drive sales. On the contrary, some will use videos as a part of their product training. In this case, videos are only posted as a way of educating the audience on how best their products can be utilized. There are numerous ways in which YouTube can be used. There is no limit to how you can use YouTube in your business.

Brand Awareness

Companies regarded as big players in the market have a unique way of using YouTube to promote their brand. A noticeable strategy that they use is that they do not focus on specific products or services that they offer. Instead, these companies market their brand in general. This leads to a scenario where customers are more aware of the brand in general, compared to specific products and services that they might be offering.

Videos that can help a company sell its brand are quite entertaining. They employ a soft-sell approach to ensure that the brand's image is cemented in the minds of their target audience. Big companies will rely on creativity to make certain that their ads stand out from the rest. Unquestionably, this is the best way of sticking out of the lot.

Product Advertising

So, if you can use YouTube to increase brand awareness, it also means that you can use it to market specific products and services that you offer. Marketing your brand and marketing the specific products and services that you offer are two different things. The approach that you use is quite dissimilar. When promoting your product, a more direct strategy will be required. This demands that you showcase the specific product that you are advertising. The uploaded video will feature the product in use and should demonstrate why the product is good for your target audience. Remember, the video should try and convince your target market why your brand is worth going for compared to rival products or services.

Retail Promotion

When it comes to retail promotion, YouTube is also a great platform to use. Experts recommend that you make use of general videos. The reason for this is that they will stay online for long without being considered as outdated. For instance, stay away from promotional videos that seek to offer discounts to your customers for a certain week or month. Doing this will only render your videos outdated within a short time. Record a video demonstrating the number of stores that you have. Show people how you manufacture and distribute your products to the different retail stores that you have. The videos could be educational. Such videos will have a long shelf life, hence helping you to avoid the process of constantly posting videos that have a short life span.

Direct Sales

Video content also stands as an ideal way of selling products and services. The videos uploaded to YouTube need to showcase the products in action. If you are offering services, a video clip showing how you offer these services will serve the purpose. The video should then end with a call to action. Direct the audience to where they can make a purchase. This could be the business website or the physical store where the services are provided.

Product Support

Not all businesses that utilize YouTube do it to win over new customers. As earlier pointed out, there are many ways of using YouTube to grow your business. In this case, YouTube can be used to offer product support to existing customers. There are common problems that customers might face when using a product. These problems can be effectively addressed with the help of a YouTube instructional video. What your business will be doing when offering these videos is helping customers to help themselves. Ultimately, your business will cut down on costs that would have been alternatively used as support costs.

Internal Training

Apart from using YouTube to reach your customers and prospective audiences, you can also use it internally. You can use it to reach out to your team. Say you have a team that works in different geographical locations. Reaching them through conventional means might be a nightmare and possibly expensive. You might want to fly to different regions to discuss how best a product could be introduced in the market. Well, thanks to YouTube, this can easily be solved. Training your employees can be done using YouTube. You need to upload a training tutorial on how a product will be introduced to the market. Anything that you would have said to your team face-to-face can be recorded and sent to them. This is how YouTube will make your life easier.

Employee Communications

Growing your business brand also requires constant communication. This communication can be made possible using YouTube. Company meetings can be held without the need for physical meetings. Your human resource manager can live stream what they would have wanted to share during a scheduled meeting and share it across the employees. Therefore, YouTube can help your brand grow by saving on time and money that would have been used to facilitate communication.

Uploading the Right Videos to Promote Your Brand

Uploading videos to YouTube is free. However, this does not mean that you should upload anything that comes to mind. It is vital that you upload videos that are not only entertaining but informative. You should post videos that your audience will like. So, what kinds of videos suit your brand? This is an important question that needs to be evaluated. Getting answers to this question will help you in knowing the right videos that you should post to guarantee that you make the most out of your marketing efforts.

Informative videos

Do you know of infomercials? Simply stated, they are advertising films that promote products or services through an informative style. Generally, they offer information about a product or service. This is how you should create your promotional videos. They should be informative. The information offered could be diverse and could feature the introduction of a new product in the market. It could also feature the business owner talking about the current industry trends. The issue here is to provide your target audience with the information they need to make informed decisions. Before hitting the upload button, consider whether the content is useful. When your customers find the information relevant and useful, the moment they want to make decisions they will think of your brand.

While working on designing an informative video, remember that your customer need not be reminded of your company. It is essential that you remember to add a good title at the beginning and the end of the uploaded video. Important information to include is your contacts and website address.

Educational Videos

Another approach that you could utilize is to create educational videos. Just as the name suggests, these are merely videos aimed at educating the audience. For instance, the video posted could take clients through how best they can use the products being advertised. In most cases, these videos will be labeled as how-to videos. They guide the audience in finding the right purpose for the products or services being sold. The main idea is to ensure that the video showcases a common thing that people know of. This will attract a large audience to your YouTube channel.

Entertaining Videos

As much as YouTube viewers expect to be educated and informed, they also expect to be entertained. Most would first want to be entertained before they can draw out your marketing message. YouTube videos should strive to win smiles from your audience. The videos uploaded should not be boring. There are various ways of selling your product on YouTube and still maintain an entertaining aspect. This calls for creativity from your marketing team. They should find ways of incorporating an entertaining aspect to the ads that will be uploaded.

Chapter 5:
Developing an Ideal YouTube Marketing Strategy

The first thing to consider before shooting any video is to evaluate how YouTube will fit into your marketing plans. Which strategy will you be using to market your products or services on YouTube? Without a doubt, you will not be posting videos blindly. You must make use of a strategy that will work for you. Ask yourself, "What do you want to achieve as you promote your products on YouTube?"

Coming up with a YouTube marketing strategy should not sound strange. This is like any marketing strategy. There are certain essential factors that you need to put into consideration. For instance, the customer comes first. Secondly, the strategy will have to consider the message. Also, it should mull over the product being sold. All these elements need to work in harmony to guarantee that you utilize an effective YouTube marketing strategy. In some cases, these elements are often referred to as the marketing mix.

This chapter will guide you through how you can develop a successful marketing strategy that will see your business thrive.

The Purpose of YouTube Videos

The first step in developing your promotional strategy is to understand the importance of the YouTube videos that you will be uploading.
Why are you uploading the YouTube videos? What is the main reason
behind using YouTube as your ideal marketing platform? What goals
do you have in mind?

Perhaps you are planning to turn to YouTube because it is what other
businesses are doing. Well, if this is what you have in mind, then it is
better not to post. As a marketing expert, you need not to do something because other people are doing it—you will never know what is
right for your business. First, sit down and evaluate the purpose of
marketing your products or services on YouTube. Your goals should
determine how you will be posting content on YouTube.

What's in it for you as you upload videos to YouTube? The chances are
that you will be helping your customers learn how to use your product. Alternatively, you might end up raising awareness about the fact
that your product could help in solving a problem. Therefore, this
could be a good reason why you want to make use of YouTube to promote what you have to offer. The main point here is that it is vital you
first determine the key thing that you need to achieve when incorporating YouTube as part of your marketing mix. As earlier pointed out,
there are various ways of using YouTube. So, don't make assumptions
that your platform will be there to entertain your audience. Have a
plan and understand the purpose as to why you wish to use YouTube.

Know Your Customer

Understanding your customer is another area that must be prioritized in developing a working marketing strategy. Who are you selling your products/services to? Also, why do you want to sell them your product or service?

As you plan to develop an effective YouTube marketing strategy, it is worth pointing out that your marketing efforts will revolve around the customer. The customer is the most important part of your business; they are the ones that will purchase whatever you are offering. If you fail to entice them, there is a certainty that your business might fail.

In a bid to know the customers you are dealing with, there are certain considerations that you need to ponder on. For example, you need to know the age of your customers. What is their gender? Where do they reside in? What do your customers do during their free time? What are some of the websites that they frequently visit? Most importantly, do they know about your product/service?

Some of these questions will help you in knowing the type of people that you will be dealing with. This guarantees that you develop a marketing plan that meets their demands. The more you know your customer, they better you are at serving them effortlessly.

Besides being informed about your customers' habits, you will also want to know whether they visit YouTube or not. It would be useless to market your products or services on YouTube, yet your target market does not visit the platform. Therefore, this is another important consideration to keep in mind as you seek to know your customer better.

Customer Tastes and Preferences

Knowing the customer's tastes and preferences will also help you in formulating a marketing strategy that will make your business prosper long term. Here, you need to take the time to understand what your target market is after. If they are regular YouTube viewers, what are they looking for? Perhaps they are looking for a specific solution to a problem that they are facing. This is where your business comes in.

Conversely, they might be browsing through YouTube to find a product that surpasses what they have been using. Your rivals might be offering similar products that are not effective, and your audience is out in search of a better brand to turn to. Knowing what your customer is after is imperative, as it will aid in formulating a marketing goal. For example, your goal here could be formulated to meet the existing need of your potential customers.

What is Being Promoted?

What are you trying to promote on YouTube? If you have been keen, then it should come to your attention that there are several things that you could be doing on YouTube. Are you trying to sell your brand? Are you trying to sell a specific product/service? What is it that you plan to market on YouTube? Certainly, from the look of things, you can't just wake up and upload videos on YouTube. You have to have a plan. This plan should include knowing exactly what you are promoting.

The main reason why you need to clear your path is to guarantee that you utilize the right strategies depending on your plan. Unquestionably, you will use different methods to sell a specific product compared to selling your overall brand. It could also be that you are out to use YouTube as a support tool. Therefore, you will not be promoting anything. This means that a different strategy will also be required when using YouTube for this purpose. How you plan to use YouTube will have a huge impact on the strategy that you will develop. Hence, it is imperative to mull over the specific things that you will be promoting.

The Message

Different messages will be utilized on YouTube depending on what is being promoted. Effective marketing demands that the message delivered to the audience should be well formulated. It is worth noting that the message will portray a picture of your brand in the minds of your audiences. Thus, creating an appropriate message is vital.

An important attribute about the message concerns what you will be telling your prospective clients about your brand. Your message should iron out the main reasons why the customers should opt for your product/service as opposed to your competitors. Why you? This is what your message should be answering. There are thousands of businesses that have channels on YouTube. Accordingly, if you need to stand out, you need to make yourself different from the rest. This is what YouTube viewers are after. They will like your channel immediately if they notice that there is something different about your message or brand. The difference could lie in how best you create your video ads. If you advert are more engaging than your competitors, you will gain a large following.

The best way of presenting your message is to sell the product/service benefits. This is what your customers are after. They need to know what makes your product/service different. If there are certain additional benefits that your competitors talk of, you need to outperform them. Marketing is all about making yourself stand out from the rest. Don't focus too much on the features that your product has. Instead, focus more on the advantages that your customers could get if they chose to rely on your product.

Measuring the Success of Uploaded YouTube Videos

After you have uploaded your YouTube video, you need to find out how it is performing. How do you do this? First, the response you get from your audience will help you in measuring whether the video was successful. What kind of response were you expecting from your audience? Did you anticipate that you will get millions or thousands of likes? If the response you get does not meet your expectations, then the video did not perform well.

Accurately measuring the success of the uploaded YouTube videos will depend on the purpose of the videos you upload. For example, if you upload a video to generate more sales, you will have to track the sales derived from the link attached to the video. If the video uploaded was meant to drive traffic to your business website, you will have to measure the resultant traffic. This can be done by measuring the number of unique visitors or the page views to your business home page. As you can see, measuring the performance of your video will depend on the purpose. So, first, understand why you are posting the videos before you can evaluate how they are performing.

Some of the basic ways of measuring the success of your videos are briefly looked at in the following lines.

Views

How often are your videos being watched on YouTube? This is an obvious way of measuring how well your videos are performing. Few views will mean that your reach is low. Perhaps you did not market your videos to different social media platforms that you have. Also, there is the possibility that your videos are not worth sharing. Find out what you are doing wrong and adjust accordingly.

Shares

To what extent is your target market sharing the videos that you are uploading? If there are minimal numbers of shares, this shows that your content might not be engaging. It is also significant to find out where your audience is sharing your content. For example, are they sharing your videos on Facebook, Instagram, or Twitter? This could be an indication that you need to market your content on these platforms. Analyzing this information helps as it gives you a map of the best social networks that you can invest in. The best part is that you will have a reason to avoid social pages that are irrelevant, depending on your customer browsing preferences.

Comments

How many comments are you getting for each video that you post? A high number of comments indicates that you are reaching many people. This is a good sign. Few comments are a red flag. Analyzing the number of views should go together with the number of comments that are being posted to your channel. Doing this will give you the insight that you need to adjust your marketing strategy.

Subscription Rate

If your content is engaging enough, rest assured that more people will subscribe to your channel. This will be an indication that your target market is interested in whatever you are selling them.

Likes and Dislikes

YouTube also has a way of letting you know immediately whether your videos are performing well or not. The number of likes you get will reveal to you how your videos are received by your audience. Many likes will give you the impression that you are doing a wonderful job.

On the contrary, several dislikes will also point out that there must be something wrong that you are doing.

Impressions

YouTube analytics will also count the impressions that you make from your posts. It should be noted that YouTube impressions do not take into consideration the number of times your viewers click on the video that you post. If your audience is impressed with the video that you post, they should leave a thumbnail on your video. Hitting like, for example, will show YouTube analytics that your content is interesting and worth displaying on pages of people that might be interested in your brand.

Chapter 6:
Grow Your Business with Facebook

To this point, it is likely that you might have tried setting up a YouTube business channel that will drive traffic to your website. Well, this is a good move that you made. Nevertheless, you should understand that these social media websites work together. YouTube alone will not guarantee you the marketing success that you crave. Therefore, you must put together Facebook, YouTube, Instagram, Twitter, and the likes.

This chapter will walk you through how you can grow your business by using Facebook. Here, you will learn more about how businesses make the best out of this platform by simple marketing strategies that they adopt.

Before diving into detail, it is important first to look at some of the main reasons why you should care about marketing your business on Facebook.

Why Marketing on Facebook Matters

One of the main reasons why you should be motivated to market your products and services on Facebook is the number of active users. Facebook boasts of having over 700 million active users. Interestingly, this number is not decreasing anytime soon. The number of Facebook users is continuously rising. Thus, it makes sense to invest in a platform that has numerous active users.

Similarly, whether your business is small or large, Facebook is an ideal platform that you should turn to. No business will claim that it is not benefiting from using Facebook to market its brand. Before overlooking the power of Facebook, think about the amount of time that people spend on this social page. Individuals could end up spending hours browsing through content on Facebook. By taking advantage of this, your business stands the chance of effectively marketing its products to its audiences.

Have you thought of the fact that Facebook is the best platform that will amplify the content that you are promoting? With the many active users, posting content on Facebook could be a great way of enticing your audience to visit other social media pages that you are active on. For instance, if you make the best of your influencers, you can rest assured that your content will be exposed to millions of people. Therefore, Facebook matters.

Wait! Targeting on Facebook is also made easy with the numerous analytic tools that you could rely on. In this case, your target audience will be ranked based on gender, age, demographics, location, interests, behavior, and their interests. Therefore, through such consumer segmentation, you will find it easy to understand your audience and meet their expectations.

Still not convinced? Multiple Facebook ad tools will give you an easier time managing your marketing campaign. The best part is that these tools are used for management purposes. By using these tools, you could effectively create and manage the Facebook ads that you will be posting from time to time.

Branding Your Facebook Business Page

Let's begin with the first step of marketing your business on Facebook. Undoubtedly, you will begin by branding your page appropriately. While trying to brand your page, it is imperative that you draw a thick line between a personal profile and a business page. These two things are different when it comes to Facebook. Profiles are personal. They are used by people to create their profiles where they could interact with family and friends.

On the other hand, pages are meant for businesses. Creating a page for your business would unlock unique Facebook features that will help you in effectively marketing your product/service. Thus, it is vital that you get it right from the first time to ensure that you do not end up creating a business profile rather than a business page.

The Facebook profile that will be created for your business should tell a story about the type of business that you conduct. It should accurately say what your business is all about and why you run your business.

Some elements worth remembering when branding your business page are discussed as follows.

The Latest Business Logo
Your Facebook business page should have the latest business logo that your business is using. The image chosen for your logo should have a high resolution and sized appropriately. Don't confuse your audience with a logo that you used ten years ago; ensure that you use an up-to-date logo that is of excellent quality.

Cover Photo
This is the image that will be used on top of your Facebook business page. Be creative enough to find an image that will appeal to your audience. For instance, the cover photo could feature your employees in action. It could be an image showing the products or services that you offer. Remember, the image used here should also be of high quality. Don't compromise on this as this will be the first thing that your audience will be viewing. Hence, the first impression is key to winning the hearts of your target audience right from the first glimpse.

Hours of Operation

If your customers are visiting your Facebook business page, they will want to find out the number of hours that you are usually open. This information should be displayed on your business page. Don't forget to mention the number of days that your store will be open. If you are normally closed on holidays, make sure that you also inform your potential clients about this.

Address

The chances are that you are running an online business as well as a conventional store. Therefore, why don't you make it easy for your clients to reach you by offering them directions on how they can reach you? An effective strategy would be to draw a map for your customers to trace the location of your physical store. Ultimately, this will increase traffic to your store.

Business Website

The main reason for using Facebook to promote your business is to increase traffic to your business page. As such, effective branding requires that you give your audience a link where they can get more information if they are interested in what you are offering. This should be your business landing page.

Products and Services

Don't forget the nitty-gritty. What are you selling? Most customers will not spend hours trying to figure out what you are selling. Therefore, make it easy for them by making it clear about the products and services that you are offering. If possible, make use of images or videos so that your customers will understand quickly more about your business.

Facebook Personality

Facebook personality defines how your business is conducted. It answers the question of who you are as a business. The business personality will be defined by the pictures, videos, and texts posts that you make. The attributes of your brand should be featured as part of your Facebook brand personality. This implies that you ought to post content that features every aspect of your business. Remember to post about your customers, employees, volunteer activities, team outings, and events that you attend.

Responsiveness

Customers expect that their queries should be answered promptly. The good thing about Facebook is that clients can post their queries directly to your help desk. In other instances, they would post their concerns publicly. Your reputation will depend on how fast you respond to them. Good customer service would be one where customer complaints and comments are responded to swiftly.

Messages are private. Nevertheless, it would be easy for a customer to determine the length of time that you took to respond to them. This implies that you ought to be fast and attend to them within the shortest time possible.

Responsiveness also requires listening. You cannot be responsive if you do not listen to your customers. They expect that you are resourceful by tending directly to their concerns. Do not end up confusing your audiences and answering questions that they did not ask. They will gain the impression that you are not responsive to them.

Relevant Content

Individuals on social media like to be associated with brands that make sense to them. They want to share posts that are not only entertaining but educative. Maintaining your current audience and attracting more to your business page demands that you post relevant content. This begins by first listening to your customers and understanding their tastes and preferences.

Content posted on Facebook should feature your business, customers, and the general industry. The message that you send to your target audience should define who you are. Your audience should not be left confused about the products and services that you offer. Similarly, they should not confuse your brand with your competitors in the industry.

Contests

There are many ways of ensuring that your audiences are constantly motivated to visit your business page. Holding contests is a good strategy to employ. Contests will add a flavor of fun to your Facebook business page. The best part is that these contests will increase customer engagement. For example, your contests could entice your audience to share content and get rewarded for their efforts. The same could be applied when encouraging your audience to subscribe to your email list. Offering discounts, for example, will motivate them to sign up to any request that you offer them.

Promotions and Sales

Promoting sales is perhaps one of the main goals of marketing your product on Facebook. What you want is for your sales to increase within the period that you are promoting your brand. Facebook is an ideal place to promote such sales. What you need is a clear photo that will direct your clients to your business home page. You should be creative in designing a photo that will motivate your customers to visit your business page. This is what most successful businesses are doing. Promoting sales will also help you in gauging whether your customers are interested in the product you offer or not. This way, you can easily plan for a sales promotion that boosts your brand visibility in the future.

Facebook Insights

As a Facebook administrator, you will have the right to use the insights section. This section provides you with the analytic data concerning the way your audience is interacting with you. For instance, you will be able to gauge their level of engagement, customer actions, page views, demographics, etc. The advantage gained in using insights is that you can easily determine the performance of your promotional campaign.

Facebook insights will help you know the best content that engages with your audience. Also, you will know the gender and age that your product impresses most. Constantly relying on Facebook insights will ultimately help you improve your Facebook campaign over time.

Chapter 7:
Developing A Facebook Marketing Strategy

We all know that Facebook is mostly used to communicate with friends, relatives, and other individuals that we perceive to be close to us. However, businesses have stepped up their game and taken advantage of the platform to market their products and services to their clients. With the high number of Facebook fans, this platform is worth investing in. A business would highly benefit because of its increased brand visibility.

However, the benefits of using Facebook as a marketing platform do not come on a silver platter. Businesses out there are investing millions in having an online presence, yet they are still struggling. Therefore, having an online presence does not necessarily guarantee that your business will thrive. What entrepreneurs need to understand is that their marketing strategies will have an impact on the success of their brands in the industry of operation.

Interestingly, the digital world is constantly changing. Thus, marketing strategies will also change periodically. This means that your marketing strategies last year might not be effective this year or the year to come. Accordingly, it is imperative that one should be flexible enough to adapt to strategies that best suit them.

This chapter will outline the best Facebook marketing strategies to make your business stand out from your competitors.

Have an Active Online Presence

Your activity on Facebook will influence the direction that your audience will be taking. If you have been keen on Facebook, you must have noticed that new content is being posted every second. This content should be digested by people before a new content pops up. Therefore, an effective strategy should feature an active Facebook presence. Do not post today and forget to post tomorrow. Your posts should be fresh and entertaining. Ensure that you upload videos and images constantly to your business page.

Growing your audience requires that you keep them engaged. To achieve this, you need quality content on your page. Undeniably, this is what they will be reading to keep themselves busy. A page that has poor content will be rarely visited and that people will not share it amongst their friends on social media.

The good news is that your efforts of remaining active on social media will pay off through an increase in your audience size. You get this at no cost. All you need is a creative plan that will post quality content to lure your audience to like and share what you post.

If at all you find a challenge in regularly posting on social media, there is a scheduling tool that you could take advantage of. This tool aids in automating the process of posting content on social media pages such as Facebook. The tool should be used in instances where you are attending to a large customer base. It is worth noting that customers expect a more personalized engagement with your brand. So, be careful not to automate everything as it will negatively affect your brand.

Make Good Use of Facebook Ads

Millions of businesses using Facebook strive to get as many "likes" as possible. Indeed, numbers never lie. Therefore, if many people like your product, it means that they love what you offer. Liking your business page will also help increase your brand's visibility as this activity will be shown in your audiences' profiles. In as much as striving to get many likes is important, you ought to focus on what matters most. Make good use of Facebook analytics to determine the customers that are mostly interested in the products/services that you offer. Such insights will also identify for you the customers that could come back and rely on your product/service repeatedly.

So, how do you reach out to these customers that are essential for your business growth? Simply said, you need to use Facebook paid ads. Yes, you heard it right; you need to make use of paid ads. Perhaps you are questioning why you should use paid ads and yet you can market your products at no cost.

The trick is that paid Facebook adverts are more effective compared to free ads. Paid ads will effectively help you in reaching your customers with ease. Accordingly, have it in mind that an ideal marketing strategy will require you to spend. Cheap is expensive. Embrace the idea of paying for your ads to get the most out of them.

Engage with Your Target Market

If you are looking to waste time on Facebook, then post content and forget about it. Rest assured that no one will comment on what you are posting. This means that your brand's visibility will likely suffer because no one is sharing or liking your content. So, don't post and forget about it. Social media is all about being social. It is a community of people and businesses brought together. Therefore, people expect that you should talk and listen to them.

Engaging with your audience entails listening to them, responding to their questions, addressing comments, and providing solutions to their existing problems. Do this, and you will see a rise in the number of followers to your business page.

When promoting your brand on Facebook, always keep in mind that you should maximize the time that your users are browsing through their pages. Consequently, it is up to you to constantly engage with them. This is the only way that they will paint a picture of your brand in their minds.

Study Your Demographics

DEMOGRAPHICS ARE AN essential part of any marketing strategy. Facebook has over one billion people actively using it. Therefore, it is important that you understand who you will be reached with your message. Also, you ought to determine how you will be reaching your audience. While studying your Facebook demographics, it should come to your attention that the audience fluctuates periodically. Therefore, you need to stay updated. Essential elements of demographics that you need to understand include:

Age and Gender

How many men and women use Facebook as their ideal social media platform? Research shows that there are more women who visit Facebook than men. Equally, individuals aged 18 – 29 mostly use Facebook. A smaller percentage of older adults use this platform.

The tip here is that you should not limit yourself to reaching only young or older adults. Facebook effectively reaches out to women and men of all ages.

Location

Knowing the location of your prospective clients is equally important. The good thing is that Facebook's reach is widely spread across all regions. However, you should strive to understand that people living in urban areas use Facebook compared to individuals living in remote locations. The wide reach of Facebook should motivate you in using this platform, where your customers come from different regions.

Scheduling Your Facebook content

If you have been browsing through different social media pages, you will notice that there is a certain way some pages are quite specific. In this case, the way you communicate on Twitter is very different from how you communicate on Facebook. With Facebook, you are at liberty to communicate anyhow without following a certain format. There are different types of content that you could post on Facebook, including stories, videos, and images. Accordingly, Facebook gifts you plenty of marketing opportunities to take advantage of.

The success of your business relies on the content quality that you post. There is a lot that people expect from your business. Thus, you should do your homework in researching more about your target audience. What do they like? What would they want to see in your posts? What do they hate?

When it comes to posting content, don't be too over promotional. Don't be too obvious. Social media demands that you bring your social nature to these networks. The last thing that people need is to talk to machines. Make your engagement more personal by posting content that is relevant to your target market.

There are different types of content that you will be posting on Facebook. Some of them are looked at briefly.

Status

In most cases, these are text messages on the wall of your business page. Your statuses need not be dull. Make good use of the wide selection of background colors that Facebook offers. This is a good way of keeping your content vibrant and appealing in nature.

Images

Posts that have images will drive more traffic to your business page. This happens because images are more engaging compared to texts. Your creativity will be displayed here. And so, your goal will be to find creative images that sell your brand. Beautiful images will oblige your audience to like your content. If you maintain the creativity over a certain period, customers will regularly visit your page to see what you have to offer.

Videos

Just like images, videos are also engaging. Facebook users constantly expect you to post educative, informative, and entertaining videos on our business page. Videos posted should be easy to understand. They should also have captions with them. Your goal is to create videos that capture your audience's attention. The idea of using a catchy headline, for example, can be a good strategy worth adopting.

Links

Besides text, images, and videos, links are another form of content that you will regularly be posting on Facebook. If you have a business website, you should make your audience aware of this by posting your website link. Links could be included within your images, texts, and videos.

Facebook Stories

These are stories that are created by Facebook users. Instagram and Snapchat are using stories to attract a large following. This feature can also be integrated as part of the posts that you will be making. Remember, you need to strive for diversity. Don't be boring by posting only images. Try out the different posts mentioned to give your audience a reason to stick around.

Posting Content at The Right Time

Finding optimal posting times is a challenge on Facebook. However, through extensive research, some marketers that have found the secret to posting at the right time on Facebook. The recommended time to post on Facebook is on Wednesday and Thursday. When posting on Wednesday, ensure that you post between noon and 2 p.m. On Thursday, the best times to post would be between 1 p.m. and 2 p.m.

Expert social media marketers argue that Thursday is the most convenient time to post on Facebook. Also, Saturday is a time when your content will least reach out to your audience. Chances are that people are busy during this time enjoying their weekend; therefore, you should minimize the rate at which you post on Saturday.

Posting early in the morning and late in the evening is also not recommended. Individuals are busy in the morning rushing to their places of work. During the evening, they are tired, and thus they would rarely spend time on Facebook.

From the information provided regarding the best times you should post on Facebook; this will affect your content engagement. Hence, it is a factor that should not be overlooked.

Tracking Your Marketing Strategy

Without tracking the performance of your Facebook marketing strategy, you will be preparing yourself for a terrible downfall. This is because you will never get to know how you are performing on this social media network. Gauging your performance is important, as it gives you a sense of direction. Moreover, it gives you an opportunity to point out the areas where you are not performing well.

Some Facebook tools will help you in tracking and monitoring your performance and discussed below.

Engagement

What is engagement? Regarding Facebook, engagement is a tool that helps you to gauge the number of times people act on your content. For instance, engagement will be gauged through the number of clicks, likes, shares, or comments. This tool is listed among the Facebook insight tools that you will be using.

Increased engagement with your content will imply that your target audience is interested in what you are offering them. Another benefit that you get from the engagement metric is that it increases your content visibility among your audiences. When Facebook notices that a certain post has been liked several times, it will surface the content to the pages of your followers. Thus, you increase the chances of getting a wider reach. But let's look at reach metric independently.

Reach

Just as the name suggests, reach refers to the number of individuals seeing your content on Facebook. This is an essential metric as it helps you determine whether your target audience is seeing your posts. Reach will also help you in gaining a deeper understanding of what your customers like. This is because there are those posts that will reach many people. Using this statistic, you can then focus your marketing efforts on reaching your audience with content that they love most.

Impressions

Impressions are closely related to 'reach.' Impressions will measure the specific number of times that a post is seen. For instance, if a certain post was seen more than once, impressions metric will note this for you. The main reason why you should measure impressions in your marketing campaign is that it gives you an insight into the viral nature of your content. If a particular post was seen more than once, this means that it could go viral. Impressions metric also aids you in knowing the rate at which your audience love what you offer them.

Referral Traffic

When you are making 'link' posts on your Facebook page, you expect that your customers will take their time to visit your business page. You need to evaluate the number of times that your link on Facebook is directing users to your business page. This will give you some insight into what works and what doesn't. If there are many referrals to your business website, this will be an indication that your content is performing well. It will reveal to you that people are sharing the content you are posting. Conversely, a low rate of referrals will be a clear indication that your content is not capturing your audience's attention as you expected. Thus, you need to create more engaging content.

Page Likes

Page likes refer to the number of individuals that like your posts. Some people might choose to follow you after liking your post. They opt to do this so that they can view your posts each time you post them. In other words, they are your fans.

The issue with page likes is that they do not accurately reveal how your marketing campaign is fairing. Undeniably, the number of likes that you have does not necessarily mean that you are performing well. There are thousands of people that simply like a page and move forward. This does not affect the product/service that you provide. Nevertheless, page likes are an important metric simply because it measures how huge your audience on Facebook is.

Video Retention

When browsing through the different videos that appear on our Facebook pages, we are often tempted to watch the videos for a few seconds before we move on. Video retention metric will help you in measuring how your audience is watching your videos. You get insights on whether they are watching the entire videos or watching for 30 seconds and leaving. With the support of this metric, you can adjust the length of your video posts to match with what your target audience expects. For example, if most of them watch your five-minute videos for only 30 seconds, then it means you need to trim them.

Click-Through Rate

You probably have done this before: seen an ad and clicked to find out more about it. Well, this is what is called the click-through rate. This metric measures the number of people that see a particular ad and take action. In this case, once your audiences see an ad, they should click for more information.

A low click-through rate implies that most people simply see your ad, but they are not taking any actions. This could happen when your ad is not relevant. Also, if your ad is boring, expect the same to happen. Facebook will also have this perception in mind. When a high number of people view your ad and do nothing about it, it means that they are less interested. Your content, therefore, does not attract attention.

So, as you can see, there are numerous ways in which you can gauge how your marketing campaign is fairing. The good thing about these tools is that some of them are added to your Facebook page and they are free to use. You need to constantly measure how you are performing. Don't walk the marketing path blindly. Don't make assumptions that you will increase your brand awareness like your competitor, who is also using Facebook to market their brand. One thing that you need to recall is that your rivals will never reveal to you their marketing strategies. Consequently, make a wise move by measuring your performance by using the Facebook analytic tools discussed.

A quick look at what you need to succeed in Facebook marketing reveals that you need to take into consideration the following tips.

Cohesive Branding
Users on Facebook expect that your brand should be consistent and that it should be different from your rival brands out there. Thus, the first step is to make your brand unique. This is achieved through proper branding on Facebook.

Be Up to Date
The secret to winning over your prospective clients is by keeping them engaged with fresh content. The updates that you make on your business page should be relevant. Keep the 80/20 rule when making posts—your posts should be 80% informative and 20% promotional.

Don't rush to yell to your audience about the products and services that you are offering. This should come out naturally through the conversation that you have with them.

Engage

Your social aspect of social media will have an impact on how your brand will perform. Try to have a dialog with your followers. Answer their questions and help them find solutions to what they are looking for. If possible, have a direct conversation with them to paint a good picture of your brand.

Call to Action

Certainly, if you are constantly engaging with your audience, you want them to act on the ads that you post. Therefore, don't forget to remind them about liking and sharing the videos and images that you are posting.

Quality Content is Key

Lastly, the quality of content posted will drive traffic to your website in all directions. Good quality will lure more people to like your Facebook business page and follow you. On the contrary, the poor quality of content will drive away traffic. Rest assured that people will not like what you are offering simply because your content is not relevant enough.

Chapter 8:
Grow Your Business with Twitter

While Twitter might not have as many users compared to Facebook, it still stands as an ideal platform that could help grow your business. Twitter stands out from all other social media pages due to its anatomy. There is a different way in which socialites interact on Twitter compared to other social media networks. Therefore, the first step to understanding how to use this platform to grow your business is to know how to use it.

A unique aspect of Twitter allows a user to use about 280 characters to send their messages. Therefore, one is limited to the number of words that their message can contain. Other important attributes of Twitter that you should be aware of are described in the following lines.

Hashtag

If you are on social media, you should know what this means. It refers to those words that are drafted to begin with a "#" sign. The main reason why hashtags are used is to classify conversations around a topic. Therefore, clicking on a hashtag will take a user to a specific page where a certain topic is discussed.

Mention

Mentions help in creating specific attention to an individual or group. By using the "@username," your message will raise the attention of the person that you are addressing. You can add several people as your mentions. Your message will reach them on their walls.

Reply

Simply stated, this is a common function that you use to respond to a tweet. Your response will be made public, and other people can see what you commented.

Retweet

A retweet is a way of showing that you like a comment on Twitter. Therefore, if a message strikes your attention, all you must do is re-tweet. For businesses, strive to have their promotional messages re-tweeted. This is an indication that they are posting relevant content that is worth sharing.

After understanding the basics when it comes to communicating on Twitter, next, you should learn how you can utilize Twitter to grow your business. Just like other social platforms, there are various ways of using Twitter to your advantage.

Build Relationships with Potential Customers

An essential strategy that you need to focus on in your social media marketing campaign is building a lasting relationship with your prospects. Twitter is a good place to do this. There is a tool that can make the entire process easy for you—the Advanced Search feature. With the help of this feature, you can search for your business prospects by using keywords. Searching with the help of this tool gives you a list of individuals or businesses that are related to the keywords you utilized.

Showcase Your Product/Service

Twitter could also be used to demonstrate your product in action. With a single animated image, you can inform your target audience about how your product is used.

Take Orders

Some businesses use Twitter to help their customers take their orders conveniently. For instance, if you are running a fast food restaurant, your customers could preorder their food without having to visit your store physically. Keep in mind that quality service provisions will determine the number of followers that will come your way. So, don't compromise on quality if at all you want a huge following.

Customer Service

Thousands of businesses are also using Twitter to offer customer service to current and prospective customers. In this case, if customers are experiencing certain challenges in using your product, solving this through Twitter is a recommended strategy. Addressing customer complaints through Twitter not only provides them with convenience, but it also guarantees that they save time. With a few tweets here and there, they could easily solve the problems they are experiencing.

Boost Engagement

One of the main goals that your business will strive to achieve on Twitter is to get many followers. Well, this might not directly imply that your business is performing well, but it will prove to you that your brand is well known. Consequently, Twitter gives you the benefit of interacting with your audience and keeping them engaged in the promotional message that you send them.

Generate Publicity

Depending on the promotional campaigns that you will be running on Twitter, your brand will gain recognition. People will be curious about your brand if they notice that it has many followers. Why are they following you? This is the question in the minds of your prospective clients. Your competitors will also want to know why your brand is popular on Twitter. But this will only happen if your ads are creative to attract a large following.

Generate User Content

Brand recognition will greatly be improved through your tweets. Twitter allows a user to post photos, videos, and texts about their products/services. With the right hashtag, you can get your audience talking about the product or service that you offer them. It is imperative that you focus on creating appealing content that will pull your target market to retweet and share.

Increase Brand Awareness

Your business will grow if you attract a large following to your Twitter business page. By frequently engaging with your clients, you get to understand them better. This, in turn, transforms into better service provision. Therefore, as people grow to love your brand, the message will spread like wildfire. As such, many people will know about the existence of your brand, and the specific products and services that you deal with.

Essential Twitter Marketing Tips for Your Business

As much as marketing on Twitter might sound like an easy bone to crack, the truth is it isn't. Simply learning the basics on how to promote your brand on Twitter will not get you to the top, nor will it get you the attention that you crave for from your customers. You need to learn more about what other businesses are doing to maintain their competitive nature in their industry of operation. Indeed, businesses that make the best out of Twitter have a large following. These companies are using Twitter to sell products and services to their clients. They are using the platform to respond to customer queries. This is perhaps their ideal platform that increases its brand awareness in the market.

But what is the secret here? What are they doing differently? This section will draft out essential Twitter marketing strategies that will ensure your business blossoms.

Make Use of Twitter Tools

To ensure that you effectively manage your Twitter marketing campaign, you will need to exploit the wide array of Twitter tools that are at your disposal. Some of the tools that you will be using include SocialRank, TweetReach, Hootsuite Analytics, etc. These tools are meant to make your marketing experience easy. For example, some of the things that you will be doing with ease include:

- Generating leads

- Finding trending subjects

- Managing your followers

- Identifying industry influencers

- Editing and adding images

Twitter tools are handy for your marketing campaign. Thus, you ought to find a way of understanding the importance of each tool that you can use.

Creating an Outstanding Twitter Profile

Part of having a good Twitter marketing strategy requires that you create an excellent Twitter profile. Unquestionably, this is your first impression. How best will you present yourself to your target market? It is vital that you create a profile that sells your brand right from the first glimpse. Your profile should entail a great bio about your business.

Twitter will allow you to use a few characters to define who you are; so, it is crucial that you maximize on selling your brand with the fewest characters possible. Every word that you use here counts.

Besides creating a great profile, you need to optimize it. Your profile should not just share the name of your business. Instead, it should reflect on your entire brand. Important considerations to be talked about include your physical location and a short description of your business.

A Twitter profile that is verified will perform well compared to one that is not verified. Verification gives customers a reason to trust your brand. This is a blue checkmark that you get after getting the appropriate verification.

Listen to Your Audience

The aspect of listening is something that you will come across in every social media marketing strategy. Customers use social media to catch up with their friends and relatives. They also use this opportunity to express their concerns about the products and services that they are relying on. All this has been made possible as businesses have turned to the internet to reach their prospective customers. As such, it is essential that you listen to what they are saying. What are they saying about your brand? Are they talking positively or negatively about your service provision? Are they out in search for a more reliable brand?

Social listening is a vital part of any successful social media marketing campaign. If you don't listen to your audience, you will not know how to serve them. Apart from listening to what your customers are saying; you should also listen to your competitors. What are they doing on social media? Which hashtags are they using on Twitter? Which promotional messages are they using often? Knowing your competitor moves helps you to differentiate yourself from their marketing strategies. Most importantly, it gives you an idea of how you could easily gain a competitive advantage by simply focusing on their weaknesses.

Create Highly Engaging Content

Any marketing expert will tell you that content is what will determine the success of your social media marketing promotion. Yes, you might be limited to just 280 words on Twitter. But this does not mean that you should waste the words you use to develop your message. It should motivate you to create highly engaging content with just a few words. The tweets that you post should resonate with your target market. Some pointers that will help you in creating great content are debated here.

Help Your Target Audience
People have all sorts of needs to be fulfilled. Consequently, you should take this to your advantage and post content that aims to solve the need they are facing. If your customers are searching for a brand that will impress them, sell your brand with the right message.

Keep It Short and Simple
Posting on Twitter doesn't mean that you should use all 280 characters given to you. Make your tweets short and simple. This will strike attention fast compared to a long tweet. Bear in mind that the audience you are reaching out to have hundreds of tweets that they need to catch up on. Therefore, get your message out with the first sentence that you use.

Make Good Use of Hashtags
The advantage of using hashtags is that it categorizes your content to make it easily accessible. This implies that it could reach out to your followers, as well as potential clients. Your audience will find it easy to reach you if you use the right hashtags. It is vital that you create short and simple hashtags that will not be confusing to your audience.

Use Multimedia Content

Videos are often preferred by social media users as they deliver information in a summarized manner. Users do not need to go through text to understand the message that you have for them. By posting an entertaining video, you will easily promote your brand. With the increased popularity of videos on social media, you should exploit this and meet your followers' expectations.

Besides posting videos to your Twitter business page, images are also a great way of communicating to your target market. Images might be less engaging as compared to videos. However, they are an effective marketing option that will also impress your audience.

GIFs are part of the multimedia content that you are strongly encouraged to use when marketing your brand. The benefit of using GIFs is that it adds some fun to your content. This means that besides posting informative content, GIFs will help you send entertaining information. If at all you do not know how to create engaging GIFs, there are numerous guides that you can find over the internet. They should help you in designing GIFs that are relevant to your marketing campaign.

Well-Timed Posting

Just like Facebook, posting on Twitter also requires that you post at the right time. With Twitter, however, your posts will not last long. The average time that a tweet lasts is only around 25 minutes. For that reason, you should post at the right time to capture the attention of your audience. To guarantee that you post timely, here are a few handy tips to help you.

Tweet Regularly

The sheer fact that tweets do not last long implies that you should post more often. Besides posting consistently, you should try to maintain an active status throughout the day. This applies mostly to situations where you are attending to customer queries.

Schedule Tweets

After posting for some time, you will notice that there is a specific trend in which your audience is responding to your tweets. With this information, you can schedule tweets. You don't have to sweat over; you could make use of Hootsuite tool. This tool will aid in scheduling your tweets in bulk, depending on how engaging your page is. Moreover, the tool can also schedule to post tweets at specific times. So, first, you need to research and understand how your audience responds.

Follow What Others are Doing

Research shows that the best time to post on Twitter would be in the afternoon. Try to schedule your posts either at noon, 5 p.m., or 6 p.m. However, this timing could change depending on the customers that you serve. As such, make sure that you adjust as per your client's timing.

Improve Your Engagement

When posting on Twitter, it is important to find ways of enhancing your engagement capacity constantly. Engagement will make a huge difference in your Twitter business page. Without engagement, you will only have thousands of followers that will not help your business grow. So, it is essential that you engage with them more often. To improve your engagement levels, here are a few tactics you should embrace.

Follow Your Followers

As you seek to attract followers, ensure that you take time to follow some of your followers. By following them, you will open yourself to learn more about their tastes and preferences.

Prompt Responses

If customers notice that you take hours to respond to them, rest assured that they might be turning to rival brands that promise them a quick response rate. As such, aim to respond to your audience within a minute. This should not be difficult for you if you have a dedicated team that attends to your tweets.

Like and Retweet

Without a shred of doubt, there is a good feeling that comes when several people like what you post. Return a similar favor to those that like and retweet your posts. Give them a reason to smile and engage more with your brand.

Ask for Help

Successful businesses that have marketed their products on social media will attest to the fact that at times they call for help from their followers. Yes, asking for help from your followers is not a bad thing. Ask them to help you build your brand by requesting their likes and shares. The more they like and share, the better your brand visibility will be. So, it won't hurt you to humble yourself and ask for assistance.

Monitor Your Brand

Monitoring your brand on Twitter demands that you take time to gauge how your brand is fairing. What are your followers saying about your brand? Are there any mentions about the product/service you offer? To effectively monitor your brand, here a few tips to mull over.

Start with Your Competitors

Your competitors will be a good source of information about the product or services that you offer. Yes, they might not mention your brand name directly, but it would be easy to determine whether they are talking about you. Also, you should listen to what your target market has to say about your competitors.

Monitor Your Keywords

The keywords that you use to create your hashtags should be carefully monitored. Take time to find out whether people are confusing your brand with a rival brand.

Listen More

Successful monitoring also demands that you listen more effectively to what's going on around your brand. Anything that touches on your brand or industry should be carefully monitored.

Chapter 9:
Grow Your Business with Instagram

How Instagram has evolved is a clear indication that the world of social media is constantly changing. Keeping up is not easy. For businesses, it means that they should be continually updated on what is happening around them. Just recently, Instagram was not popular. Most people used this platform to post their selfies. It was not something serious until businesses realized its potential.

With the increased number of businesses that turned to Instagram for their marketing needs, Instagram stepped up and incorporated marketing tools that would help businesses achieve their goals. Key performance indicators were included within the platform. At first, the platform helped businesses to increase their brand visibility. However, with time this developed into a fully-fledged marketing platform.

Marketing on Instagram has no bias to the industry where you might be running your business. It is imperative to take advantage of the online presence that Instagram offers your company. To ensure that you make the best out of Instagram for your business, you ought to know the ins and outs of using this platform to market products and services. This means that you have to learn more about the type of content that you should post here and the recommended ways of developing a marketing strategy. After learning the basics, you must learn how best to monitor your performance with the help of the metrics offered on the platform.

The first thing that we will take into consideration is to know how your post will perform on this social media platform. The issue here is to determine the number of people that will see your Instagram post. Here is a look at five essential factors that influence the performance of your post.

Engagement

Posts that have a high number of likes, shares, views, and comments will rank highly as compared to others. Just like Facebook, when a post receives thousands of likes, it signals the Instagram algorithm that the post is of great quality. In other words, Instagram will quickly identify this post as engaging. Therefore, the post will be shown to many users since it will highly likely impress many.

However, there are instances where the Instagram algorithm will overlook the number of shares, likes, or comments. In other cases, the algorithm will only consider how fast the post engages with your audience. To circumvent any issues from arising with the Instagram algorithm being utilized, you should embrace the idea of scheduling posts. While doing this, time is of the essence. Make sure that you schedule the Instagram posts at the right time to reach your target market effectively. This increases the chances of reaching out too many people.

Time Spent on Your Post

The Instagram algorithm will also focus on evaluating the length of time your users spend on the content that you post. This algorithm works in the same way as Facebook's algorithm does. What does this mean to you as a marketer? You need to be creative and come up with engaging content. Your Instagram posts should be captivating to keep your audience glued to them.

Favorite Accounts

When engaging with Instagram using a certain account frequently, it reports to the Instagram algorithm. It shows it that you love the content being posted. Consequently, Instagram steps in to display similar content that would be relevant to you. This is what you should bear in mind when posting to your Instagram business page. Step into the shoes of your audience, and you will understand what they expect from you. It will help you in determining the most relevant content for your audience.

If your audiences keep commenting and liking your posts, Instagram will work to ensure that other posts for your business are displayed on the pages of your audiences. This is a secret that will ultimately help you in becoming a good marketer on Instagram.

Timeliness of A Post

The Instagram algorithm will also take into consideration the time that a post was created. This means that the algorithm will arrange the posts based on how recently they were uploaded. Therefore, if you fail to keep your posts updated, your audience will rarely see them on their feeds. So, forget about posting once a week. Find time to schedule fresh posts as it warrants that the algorithm highly ranks your content.

Type of Content

The content genre will play a huge impact on what will be displayed on the feeds of your audiences. For instance, if your audience keeps searching about sports highlights, more content about sports highlights will be displayed on their Instagram walls. This is where the aspect of relevance comes in. The type of content posted will determine whether it's relevant or not. Knowing the right content to post begins with understanding your audience. Who are they and what are they looking for?

Designing Your Instagram Profile

With the increase in Instagram's popularity, the platform has grown to become an essential part of any business' marketing strategy. It is for this reason that designing a good Instagram profile matter. What does your profile say about your brand? Does it feature your business' bio? Is the profile visually appealing? These are a few of the questions that should ring in your mind as you take a closer look at your Instagram business profile.

The profile that you use will determine whether you will make a lasting impression in the minds of your audiences. A good impression will lure your audience to hit the like or share button right away. Through the content that you share, you can gradually transform those likes into loyal followers of your brand.

Optimizing Your Bio

To stress the importance of a good Instagram business profile, your bio will tell a lot about your business. But first, ensure that your profile has a business look rather than a personal look. Your prospective clients should not be confused about whether your account is for business or personal purposes.

Using a business Instagram is a fundamental step to ensuring that you gain access to features that will help you in promoting your brand. Some of these features that are included in a business profile include Instagram insights, contact button, and promoted posts. One thing that you should realize here is that it is not a must that you opt for a business profile. However, it is highly recommended because it comes with numerous benefits that will eventually help you. Important considerations to bear in mind when optimizing your bio include:

- Your business backgrounds

- Your branded hashtag

- Keywords

- Call to action

- Your business emails

- Website link

Instagram Stories

A perfect Instagram marketing strategy should include Instagram stories. If you have used Snapchat before, you will understand what "Instagram stories" is all about. "Instagram stories" refers to a feature that you will find within the Instagram application, giving users the ability to create a story by bringing together different images or videos. This is a secret that most businesses have discovered and are using this feature to their advantage.

The success of "Instagram stories" is greatly influenced by the popularity of visual content on social media pages. Tons of businesses have noticed that there is an increased consumer engagement when visual content is used. Consequently, the Instagram feature is gaining attention each day.

Some features of "Instagram stories" that will help your business grow its brand include:

Instagram Stories Links

Businesses can now enjoy the fact that they could easily add links to the stories that they create. Earlier on, this feature was not available. The good news here is that businesses get to share their stories with thousands of their followers by sharing the links to such stories. This sharing will certainly be a good driver of traffic to your business page.

Instagram Stories Highlights

The highlights feature is also another attribute of Instagram stories that will make a difference in your business profile. The best clips are assembled and displayed on your bio. Therefore, you can easily create a lasting impression by choosing clips that tell amazing stories about your business. Think of the highlights as a movie trailer. Most people will be tempted to watch a movie after watching its trailer. Interestingly, the film might not be as captivating as the trailer but what matters most is the convincing power of that trailer. Do you get the point? Highlights will help you market your business with ease as you could easily entice new followers to depend on your brand.

Location and Hashtag Stories

Stories on Instagram here feature the specifics such as the location or the hashtag used in creating the stories. The location where the story is created will be tagged alongside the Instagram story. Hence, if the story is created around your business premises, other related stories will show up when a user searches for your premises. What does this mean for your business? It infers that your business will gain more exposure.

Instagram Live

Instagram live will give your business an opportunity to going live. Well, with Instagram stories, you can upload recorded videos and images. This means that you have time for retakes. However, this is different from Instagram live as you don't have time for retakes. The best thing about this attribute is that it could aid in boosting your business growth if used appropriately. This is what customers love. Hence, there is a good chance that it will lead to enhanced consumer engagement.

Having the right strategy when planning to use Instagram live in your business will help you achieve your business' marketing goals. When using Instagram live, you have the freedom of exploring your creativity. Nevertheless, you can't do things blindly without having a plan. So, here are some tips on using Instagram live that you ought to consider.

Use It to Launch New Products

Because you will be live, it is a great tool to introduce new products to your target audience. This implies that you have the freedom of showcasing the different aspects of your product. Alternatively, you could tease your audience with a future product that will be introduced. All these will create excitement that will surround your brand.

Collecting Emails

You could also spice things up by using Instagram live to collect emails. The first step you should take is to request your followers to send in their questions via email. Collecting emails via Instagram live gives your business a personalized touch.

Promoting Sales

You are live, so it could be wise to take advantage of this and promote sales through Instagram live. For example, work on promotions that last for a short period. This will attract a large following since you are offering huge discounts to the products/services that your customers depend on. Such promotions will go viral thereby enhancing your brand visibility.

Instagram Influencer Marketing

Influencer marketing continues to grow on social media. This is given a huge boost by the fact that customers get to make their decisions after being influenced by those that they trust. Businesses use this to their advantage and rely on influencers to market their brands. It is for this reason that Instagram influencer marketing is also a promotional strategy worth adopting. It is highly effective for business growth as it brings in the aspect of trust to your marketing campaign. It breaks down barriers of conventional marketing as customers are introduced to brands from trusted sources. Influencers work similarly as friends do. Just as a friend could recommend a product or service, influencers have a similar impact. Consequently, it becomes easy to market your brand to your followers as they trust their sources.

The process of finding reliable influencers on Instagram might be a daunting task—more so if you are going to do this for the first time. Nevertheless, considering these few tips will give you a roadmap to settling for the right influencers.

Consider Their Instagram Engagement

How well is the influencer engaging with their audiences? If the influencer has a high engagement rate, then it means that their followers act to the content that they post. Generally, what your business needs is to rely on influencers with a high engagement rate. This will assure you that their followers will have a positive influence on your brand.

Consider the Quality of Followers

Besides mulling over the engagement rate of the influencer you plan to choose, you also need to consider the quality of their followers. Are these people interested in your product/service? You need to align yourself to influencers that have an audience that directly relate to what you offer. For instance, if you are selling sports gear, your influencer should have followers interested in sports gears. This implies that by relying on such quality of followers, you increase the chances of boosting your brand's visibility.

Budget

Some businesses prioritize this factor when making decisions on whether to depend on influencers or not. Undeniably, the amount of money that they require for their services will have an impact on the direction that you will take. If they are costly, the chances are that you should consider finding other reliable but affordable influencers. Some influencers will charge you based on the sales that they bring to your business. Others will consider the leads they create. So, it is imperative that you get to know how much they charge before making your final decision.

Number of Followers

The number of followers that a social media user has does not necessarily mean they have a high engagement rate. There are some users with thousands of followers, but their engagement rate is low. Even so, it still makes a lot of sense to think over the number of followers that your influencer has. A huge following will give you the impression that your brand will easily reach out to a huge audience.

Instagram Advertising

Whether you plan to increase sales or attract new audiences, it is important to utilize Instagram advertising. Creating your Instagram advert is not difficult. The good news is that there are tons of guides for you to turn to over the internet. Your ads could feature photo ads, boosted posts, carousel ads, video ads, and ads on Instagram stories.

Tracking Instagram Success

Tracking your performance is not the last thing that should come to your mind; it is an activity that should be done regularly. You need to track how your content performs. Whether you are tracking specific content, it is important to know what works for your business and what needs changing. For instance, you might want to find out whether your videos are performing well as compared to the images that you post. Generally, by continuously tracking your Instagram success, you will find ways of improving on the content that you deliver to your audience.

Several metrics will make the job easy for you. Some of these metrics are like metrics used in other social media pages. Regardless, it is still imperative to know how to use them.

Reach

Reach will help you in measuring the number of people that saw your post or ad. This metric can help you in narrowing down to the unique viewers that accessed your content.

Impressions

Just like the reach, impressions will help you get insight into the number of times your post has been seen. How is your audience interacting with your post? Impressions will help you get the numbers on how they are clicking through your Instagram business page.

Engagement

THIS METRIC WILL MEASURE the number of people that have commented, liked, or shared your posts. The metric will only measure the number of unique accounts. Therefore, if a single individual liked your post ten times, this will be counted as one.

Engagement Rate

Engagement rates give you information regarding the percentage of viewers engaging with your content. This will be calculated by an Instagram algorithm. It divides the number of comments and likes by your total number of your followers.

Follower Growth

As a marketer, you need to find out whether your following is growing or not. Therefore, with the follower growth metric, you get to gauge the number of new followers that you get on your social media page. The analysis will be done depending on time. It could be a week or a few months. This information will help you in understanding how best your brand or Instagram account is growing.

With the anticipated growth of Instagram, it is important than ever before for your businesses to use the platform to market its products or services. But first, it begins by understanding how Instagram works. This entails learning how to market your brand using

Instagram tools effectively. Moreover, you also must evaluate what works for your business. This is made easy with the help of analytic tools that are at your disposal. Your business needs a unique online presence that will make it stand out from other rivals in the market. Other businesses have their online presence, too; accordingly, you should not be left out as this is what makes businesses remain competitive in the industry.

Chapter 10:
Converting Followers into Loyal Customers

One of the most important social media marketing goals is to pull many followers. However, this is not enough to guarantee that your business will thrive. It takes more than having thousands of followers liking and sharing your content. After completing the first step of winning over followers, you need to take a step further and convince them that you are the right brand. This is another fundamental step that you should bear in mind in your social media marketing campaign.

Without conversion, your social media marketing efforts will be useless. It is pointless to spend millions on trying to lure followers to like and share your brand, yet they do not fully depend on it. It is imperative that you work on conversions. Conversion is as important as creating engaging content on social media.

So, what do you do to guarantee that you convert your followers into loyal customers? If this is something that you have been pondering about, worry no more. This section will take a deep dive in helping you understand the best ways of increasing your social media conversion rate. Note that the strategies proposed here will apply to any social media page that you might opt to use.

Invest in Research

The first step to turning your followers into loyal customers begins with understanding them. You need to know your followers. This, therefore, demands that you should spare some time to find out about their needs and preferences. Well, this might change often, but you must know what makes their hearts melt. If your followers have certain challenges, ensure that you identify this early. You might also want to know what your followers do for a living.

But, why is this research important? Reason number one is that you will better understand how to deal with your audience. Knowing them gives you the advantage of personalizing your connection.

Secondly, doing your research helps you to paint a picture of your ideal client. This means that you will continuously find ways of impressing them through the products/services that you offer.

Analyze Your Content

By now, we are assuming that you are using several social media pages to market your brand. This implies that you are making use of Facebook, Instagram, YouTube, Twitter, etc. to promote your brand. After gaining the followers that you have been looking for, the next thing would be to win them over. Converting them into loyal clients of your brand should be considered as an important step.

A strategy that works is to analyze your content properly. Take time to consider the social media pages that send the highest sales leads. Compare the different type of posts that you often make, which among them stands out from the rest. Besides this, your analysis will also include the process of finding out the right times that you should be posting content.

If things are not working for your business, find out why your content is not delivering as you had anticipated. Analyze your content with the help of the social media tools provided in every social media network. The data you obtain from social media tools are not mere numbers. They are essential information that will guide you in strengthening your social media presence.

Tempting Your Followers

A marketing rule of thumb that you should always have at your fingertips is never be too pushy. The goal of marketing is to persuade customers to depend on your product or service. Remember, it is not a must that they turn to your brand. However, your main aim is to convince them that you are the right brand that will meet their demands.

So, what do you do? Tempt them. Yes, tempting your audience will have them thinking about your brand more often. Give them content that will keep them tempted on why they should choose you over your competitors. A recommended tip here is to create stories. The good thing is that this is easy to achieve more so on Facebook and Instagram. Make up a story that will influence their buying decisions and that they will remember it along the way.

Another tip that could work is to entice your followers by giving them offers worth turning to. Create a contest to engage them. Convince them that if they purchase a certain product, they stand a chance of winning something. This could be tickets to a particular game or vouchers. Your customers will be tempted to go for your offers since there is something good for them. The best part is that through their regular participation, you will increase your brand awareness besides the fact that you will be converting them into loyal customers.

The most important thing is to be innovative. It is essential to give your followers a reason to remember you the next time they want to purchase the product that you offer.

Develop a Personalized Contact

Who doesn't fancy the feeling that comes with being considered as a special person? We all love to feel appreciated for our actions. People crave attention, and this is what your business should capitalize on. A simple follow-up message to your customers remembering their birthday will create a lasting impression. The point here is that you should create personalized content for your followers. While doing this, don't forget to add a call-to-action message that demands low commitment from your audience. Try your level best to create a message that is specific to your audience's interest. It makes them understand that you know more about them. Therefore, your conversion rate will gradually increase.

Embrace the Act of Giving

As you seek to convert your followers into customers, you should remember that your content will keep you engaged. Certainly, you cannot convert followers if at all you have nothing to offer them. Social media users rely on social media for entertainment. Your goal is to surpass their expectations by offering them quality content.

Great content should feature interesting aspects of your product/service. Keep things entertaining by being creative. For instance, you could spice things up by requesting your audience to post their recommendations on how your next line of a product should be packaged.

Delivering beyond your customer expectations is what will make them place your brand at the front of their minds.

Find a Balance

With the numerous social media pages that your business will be relying on, choosing the best might be confusing. Your business should make use of several social media pages, as this guarantees you maximize the benefits that accrue in marketing your brand on social media. Consequently, besides using Facebook, you should also use Instagram, Twitter, YouTube and other platforms that you deem necessary.

The challenge that you will likely face is that of finding the right balance on the social media pages to use. A vital step to converting your audience into loyal customers begins by determining the right social pages that work for you. Several social media tools should help you in knowing this. It is likely that the best social media website will be that which drives high traffic to your business website.

Loyalty

Your business will undoubtedly get the best out of loyal fans and followers. Putting fans and followers together transforms into loyal customers. Nevertheless, one good turn deserves another. So, for your customers to be loyal, you must take the first step.

Maybe you are wondering how you can show loyalty. Simply said, you need to be consistent and show concern to your audience. Accordingly, meet your audience expectations by posting quality content regularly. Don't forget that the content should also be relevant.

If you are going to be away for a while, inform your followers. Keep them updated on everything that you plan to do. This is being loyal to your customers. In turn, they will also be loyal to your brand.

Rely on Testimonials

Don't blow your own trumpet just yet let your customers do the job for you. Instead of focusing on mentioning the good things that you are doing for your business, focus on improving your products/services. After selling your product to an esteemed customer, request them whether they could leave their comments behind on your Facebook business page. Their comments will end up motivating other users to turn to your brand.

Equally, the idea of sharing testimonials aids in reminding your target audience of the products that you offer. Most importantly, it signals to other socialites that your brand is promising and valuable.

Chapter 11:
Social Media Marketing Dos and Don'ts

Posting on social media can be exciting—more so if you are marketing your brand for the first time. However, it should be noted that there is a lot that goes into social media marketing. From what you have read, there is a lot that you need to digest before you can argue that you are a good social media marketer. Besides learning the art of social media marketing is a continuous process. This is because the world of social media is constantly evolving. What you thought is a good marketing tool might not be efficient tomorrow. So, it is wise to be flexible in how you use social media to market your brand.

Many businessmen will get confused about what they should do when marketing their products/services on social networks. This is logical. There is a lot to be learned, and that cannot be done overnight. There-fore, cut yourself some slack if you are not aware of the do's and don'ts when marketing your brand on social media. Luckily, this sec-tion will help you find answers on this matter.

Do Fill Your Business Profile Fully

To ensure that your social media activity is in order, beginning with the most important things first: filling out your business profile. Depending on the platform, this might take some time. Twitter, for example, is quite easy to complete your business page. All you need is a detailed bio, a good profile picture that showcases your brand logo, and a link to your business website. On the contrary, Facebook requires more information on your wall.

It is essential that you fill out all social media pages with accurate information regarding your brand. This does not imply that you should copy and paste data from one page to the other. Yes, the content should be similar, but it does not mean that the language used should match all through. Be creative and create similar profiles with the same message.

Do Use Automation Software

So, its 4 p.m. and you are busy attending a meeting. Should you postpone posting on your social media page? Certainly, this is a question that most people will want to be informed about.

There are times when you will be held up and that you will have no time to post content on social media. For instance, you cannot be awake every time at 3 a.m. to post content. What should you do? This is where the use of automation software comes in. The software will help you in scheduling posts without being there physically.

Therefore, you will conveniently post content on your social networks without interrupting your schedule.

There are all sorts of automation software on the internet. Some of them are free, whereas others cost money. Regardless, ensure that you settle for software that suits your business marketing goals.

Do Share Relevant Content Without Fear

By now you should have gained an overall perspective of why posting relevant content is vital for successful social media marketing. However, there are those days when you will feel that you have nothing to post. This happens. There are times when you will run out of ideas. One thing about posting is that you should not just post anything. Your audience has a huge expectation, and, thus, you should think twice before posting anything.

In line with posting content, it doesn't also mean that you should go for days without making any posts. Posting regularly is a requirement that guarantees the success of your social media promotion. If you are out of ideas, consider finding out what your competitors are doing. It should give you an idea of what you should post to keep your audience engaged.

Do Respond to Comments and Questions

Now that you know how to engage with your audience fully, there is a possibility that questions and comments will stream in. If you have a large customer base, then there are instances when comments and questions will overwhelm you. One thing that you should understand is that it might not be possible to respond to all your followers. Therefore, you need to determine the responses that you should prioritize first. For example, questions from your audience would be regarded as more pressing compared to comments. If complaints are part of the responses that you are getting, address them first. Afterward, attend to comments.

Ultimately, your customers will be happy that their voices are being heard. They would feel appreciated and this will contribute to increased customer engagement.

Do Make Posts on Your Own or Hire an Expert

There are numerous times that we have heard on the news about an intern tarnishing the reputation of a company through erroneous posts. Making mistakes on social media is a risky thing. This is because news spread quickly on social media. It is essential that when making posts, you are posting on behalf of the entire company. Thus, mistakes must be avoided completely.

Wrong posts that do not reflect what your business is all about will hurt your brand. The worst could happen as you could end up being the news headlines. If you can't do the posting, hire an expert to do the job. They should have relevant marketing experience to warrant that they know what they are doing.

Don't Be Too Salesy

Each time you are promoting your brand on social media, you should bear in mind that there are hundreds of other businesses doing the same. This means that your audiences are constantly exposed to promotional content. You are not the only business seeking to turn audiences into loyal customers.

So, begin by understanding what your customers need. Don't start yelling to your prospective clients about the products and services that they could turn to. People use social media to communicate. Businesses are just lucky that they can use these platforms to promote their brands. Consequently, don't make your business profile to look like a conventional store. Entice your audience with videos and images that do not necessarily talk about your brand. It could be something funny that you want to share with them. The trick is to keep your target audience engaged.

Don't Post Robotically

Customers depending on your brand will expect a conversational tone from you. They do not want to talk to robots about the challenges they are facing when using your product. Accordingly, you should work to make certain that your posts have a human voice. They should be optimized to suit your customer queries. This way, your clients garner the feeling that your business is listening to them. Put yourself in the shoes of your audience. What would you expect from a company that you depend on? Without a doubt, you expect them to communicate to you in a human way. You don't expect to be connected to automated replies that appear robotic. It's certainly not a good feeling. Therefore, play your part by making sure that you focus on replying comments in a naturally.

Don't Focus on Negative Comments

As formerly mentioned, it is not possible to respond to all your followers. What you need to do is prioritize the responses that need urgency. Complaints, for example, they should be attended to first. Comments can wait. In line with this, you should always remember that it is impossible to please everyone. So, expect negative comments here and there regardless of the efforts you put to improve your product/service.

While dealing with negative comments, you might be tempted to delete them from your social media business page. Well, don't do this. Deleting negative posts will raise a red flag. It will tarnish the good reputation that you might have built for a while now.

Don't Post Text Only

If you are trying to bore your audience to death, post text only. Your followers need diversity. They need text, yes; but they also need images and videos. Diversity in your content will lure your audience to maintain a high engagement rate. It is for this reason that businesses are advised to have different social media pages. This is because the content posted on Facebook will automatically be different from what is posted on YouTube. Thus, there is some form of variety that your followers can enjoy.

Don't Overlook Other Social Accounts

Besides Facebook, Twitter, YouTube, and Instagram, there are tons of other social media pages that your business could turn to. With the popularity of some of these social networks, it is easy to get side-tracked. You might end up focusing too much on Facebook and forget to market your product or service on Instagram. This is a common thing that happens. However, as a good marketer, you should not overlook other social media accounts. Remember, different social media pages will reach out to a varying audience. Hence, balancing your marketing equation is vital.

Don't Forget To Post On Time

As earlier mentioned, there are specific times that you should post on your social networks. Proper timing will guarantee that you post when your audience is active. For that reason, always stick to posting at recommended time intervals for optimal social media marketing results. Don't Mix Personal and Business Profiles

If you are going to market your business on social media, confirm that you have separate accounts for your personal and business use. Don't use your Facebook page to post your personal issues. The individuals that are following your brand do not want to be told about how you spent your weekend with family. Keep your private issues private.

Use your business profile for business use only. This way, your followers don't feel bothered by your personal space.

Don't Be Unprepared for Complaints

Complaints will always be there. You cannot start a business without expecting to fail at some point. While marketing your brand on social media networks, expect people to complain. They will have negative comments about your product or service. As a wise businessman, the best thing you can do is to be ready for those comments. How will you deal with them? If you are not sure about how best you can deal with negative comments, seek help. The point is that you should not make matters worse by bringing in personal feelings.

Don't Push Your Followers to The Edge

Interestingly, you would not try asking someone to marry you the first time you meet. In the same way, you should not push your audience to the edge. Give them time to grow with your brand. Help them where necessary. Comment, like and share their comments where possible. However, don't nag them asking them to share or like your content. This will appear too pushy and desperate. Give your followers a reason to believe that you trust your brand. As such, let things take its course as you focus on improving your marketing strategies from time to time.

Don't Rush Things

There are those brands that get lucky while marketing on social media. In a few weeks' time, they rise to become top rated brands. Well, this rarely happens. You need to understand the fact that it takes time to win the trust of your clients. Effective marketing on social media is all about developing a momentum. Tackle each day at a time for the best results.

Chapter 12:
Common Social Media Marketing Challenges

Marketing Challenges

As we try and look at the bright side of using social media to promote your brand, we cannot turn a blind eye on the common challenges faced by businesses. Businesses are accustomed to conventional marketing strategies. Therefore, making the best of social media isn't as obvious as you might have thought. Marketing goals might be similar, but the strategies to be used are different.

There are several common challenges that businesses face as they use social media to promote their brands. Any marketing strategy will certainly face periodically. As such, you should not be discouraged the moment you realize that your content is not working for you. Let's take a closer look at some common challenges that will come your way as you strive to promote your brand on social media.

Developing the Right Social Media Strategy

It comes as no surprise that developing the right social media strategy would be the main challenge you might face. Social media strategy refers to a description of the plan that you will be using to promote your brand on social media. Coming up with a well laid out strategy is not an easy task. So, how do you go about dealing with this challenge?

The first step that you need to work on is to list down your goals and objectives. While doing this, try to be specific on what you need to achieve out of this social media campaign. Take a closer look at your goals. Are they attainable? Setting unrealistic goals will only demoralize you. Thus, it is advisable to set goals that can be attained within a short period. They will motivate you since you are trying to get the ropes on how to successfully market products and services on social media.

Measuring ROI

Social media ROI refers to the returns on investment that your business gains from using social media marketing. Undeniably, after using social media marketing for some time, you will want to know whether your time and money paid off. The challenging bit of measuring ROI is the fact that it could be difficult to determine how the social media pages are paying off accurately. For example, it can be difficult to determine the value of your tweet right away.

Your social media returns on investment should align with the goals and objectives of your business. This implies that your social media ROI will differ from those of your rivals. Measuring ROI, therefore, requires that you have a clear set of marketing goals and objectives.

This boils down to the marketing strategy. Having the right plan on how you will conduct your social media campaign will help you in effectively measuring what you get back from your investment.

Converting Employees into Brand Advocates

There are times when social media marketing will require you to use your big guns to become successful. Often, you will be focused on your product and customers. From time to time, you will think that the most important thing to do would be to generate awareness and increase brand visibility. Well, this is not a bad thing to focus on. There are multiple areas that you will have to focus on; hence, it could be confusing. At some point, you will forget the importance of your employees in the marketing campaign. They are an essential part of your promotion. They are the individuals that could best define your product as they understand it perfectly.

About the above, converting employees into brand advocates might be a daunting task as this could be the last thing that you have in mind. To ensure that they are your brand ambassadors, make sure that they are sharing good content to your followers. They should educate your followers on how to use your product and respond to any complaints accordingly. Once you feel that your employees are your brand representatives, you can be confident that your brand will gain a positive image in the market.

Deciding the Right Social Network To Use

Over 2 billion folks use social media today. Over 70% of these people use social media to make their buying decisions. What's more, 90% of social media users interact with the brands that they rely on. Keeping these statistics in mind, it should be obvious to you that your business should have an online presence. However, this is where things get confusing. There are tons of social media pages over the internet. If you are not careful, you might end up settling for social networks that do not work for your business.

Nevertheless, this challenge is easily solved by simply understanding the audience that you are targeting. Who is your audience? Which social media pages are people most active on? Do they use Facebook, Twitter, Instagram, or YouTube more often? These are some of the inquiries that should ring in your mind as you think over your audience.

Before choosing any platform, you should first study your audience. Fortunately, several tools will help you in knowing the audience that you are dealing with. Social media tools that are made available to you will help you in knowing where your audience is located, what they are after, which social media pages they are active on and what content entices them the most. So, make sure that you rely on social media analytics tool to understand your audience as this is a fundamental step that will guide you to choosing the right social media network.

Declining Organic Reach

After devoting a lot of time and money to promoting your brand on social media, you expect good results. However, this might not come as easily as you think. Your posts might not reach out to your audience as effectively as you had planned. This is a common thing that happens, and thus, you should not be discouraged.

It is important to note that there are thousands of people and businesses posting content to their social media pages. Therefore, it might be a challenge to ensure that your posts stand out. To solve this issue, the quality of your content will matter greatly. Appropriate tracking will be required to determine the performance of the different posts you will be making. Hence, you should evaluate the posts that are performing well and those that are lagging. For example, you might end up noticing that video posts are performing better than texts. As such, you should focus on creating more video posts rather than texts—it all depends on what your audience needs.

Promoting Your Brand in A Regulated Industry

The amazing thing about social media is the fact that it allows all kinds of businesses to promote their products and services. Nonetheless, there are industries with serious regulations that might hinder you from promoting your product on social pages. Take for example the alcoholic beverages industry. Certain regulations will prevent you from freely marketing your brand.

In such cases, what you need to do is to understand your industry of operation. Take time to learn about the rules and regulations governing the marketing of products in that industry. Being conversant with these regulations certifies that you don't end up crossing the line and ultimately affecting your brand.

Humanizing Your Promotion

In as much as thousands of people will follow your brand, the interesting thing is that most followers are annoyed with promotions on their social networks. The point here is that your presence on social media should not be based on just selling your products or services. Succeeding on social media marketing requires that you also take a humanistic approach to understand your followers.

To deal with this challenge, you ought to embrace the idea of storytelling. By telling stories to your prospective clients, you will be revealing to them about your company values indirectly. Therefore, you give your audience a reason to stick with you. The advantage gained in using stories is also the fact that you will instill brand loyalty amongst your followers.

Your responsiveness will also help you in solving this challenge. Act like a human and respond to them fast. Take time to reach back to your followers by responding to their comments and liking their posts where necessary. This is what any human being will do. So, do the same.

Answering All Questions

It is always a challenge to attend to all your followers. If you are deal-ing with a large audience, this even becomes a problem. Well, the good news is that social media pages have got tools that will help you in managing your content effectively. A good example of a tool that you can and should use is Sprout Social. This tool will make sure that new messages do not go unattended to. It puts all your social media pages in one place. Hence, it is easy for you to answer them without having to log in to each social media website.

Hiding messages that you have attended to is a great way of confirm-ing that you only pay attention to those that are not answered. This is something that Sprout Social can also help you with.

Tracking Results

Marketing on social media is a tricky game. Having many followers might not necessarily mean that you will be running a successful business. Equally, your impression stats might not mean that you will be making huge sales. It is a daunting task to track the results of your marketing campaign accurately. You should know that your ad on so-cial media could take up to months for it to be effective. Yes, your followers might be impressed today, but they will make their purchas-ing decisions the following month. So, it calls for patience from your end.

Tracking results effectively demand that you make good use of social media monitoring tools. Some of these tools are free to use whereas others are paid versions. You should utilize tools that are commonly used by other businesses. More on this will be discussed in the next chapter.

Besides using management tools to track results, you should also break down your data into meaningful information. For instance, after learning about your clients purchasing behaviors, you should break this down to their specific need. In this case, you might want to schedule posts at a time to boost your reach.

Generally, challenges will be part of your social media marketing. There is no guarantee that you will sail through the marketing process without facing any obstacles. Understanding how to deal with them is crucial. It motivates you to move in the right direction. Challenges are not meant to discourage you. They are there to strengthen you and ascertain that you are fit to overcome any hurdles that might come your way. So, brace them with your marketing expertise.

Chapter 13:
Handy Social Media Marketing Tools

We have talked about the fact that your business will need more than one social medium marketing platform. Different social media pages will have varying influences on your marketing campaign. LinkedIn, for example, will bring you slightly different followers from Pinterest or Facebook. You need to have an online presence on social pages that are popular. Consideration should also be based on what your target market uses frequently.

Managing all these social media networks is an overwhelming task. There is a lot that needs checking and constant updating. It is for this reason that social media marketers are often advised to use social media monitoring tools to help them handle the management task. This section will walk you through some of the most important social media marketing tools. Understanding how to use them warrants that you find the entire marketing experience to be stress-free.

Hootsuite

Hootsuite is a management tool that brings all your social media pages to one dashboard. Therefore, you don't have to visit all your social media pages from different tabs to manage them. With the help of this tool, your management process is made easy. Thus, scheduling your posts is not as difficult as you thought.

Buffer

Buffer will help you deal with your posts. If you have several posts that you need scheduling Buffer will do the job for you. It doesn't matter where you need to post your content. Whether you are looking to post on Twitter, Facebook, LinkedIn, etc., Buffer will schedule the posts for you. Moreover, part of its unique features is that you also get the opportunity of reviewing the posts that work and those that don't. Hence, with time you will improve as you learn how to create engaging posts.

Lithium

With Lithium connecting with your followers will be possible. The tool also aids in automation of posts to different social media pages. Equally, the tool can also be used to monitor your conversations with your followers. Through effective monitoring, you can be sure that you will enhance your customer engagement capacity.

Sprout Social

This is a tool that has been talked about earlier on. If you are looking to humanize your promotion, this is the tool that you should be using. It helps you deepen existing connections with your followers. Sprout

Social achieves this through how it assists in maintaining effective communication.

Keyhole

Part of your social media marketing requires that you understand what matters to your audience most. Keyhole is a tool that will give you insights on what your followers fancy. Thus, you can easily create content that will generate attention. The tool will also reveal to you the time when your followers are most active. This means that you can adjust your posting times to guarantee that you increase your reach and engagement rate.

Reputology

Monitoring social media reviews is a crucial aspect of social media marketing. You need to know what your customers are saying about your brand. With the help of this tool, such monitoring is made easy. If there are bad comments regarding your brand, you will find ways of solving them before they tarnish the reputation of your company. Well, it is not just about monitoring negative reviews. Reputology will also aid in catching those positive reviews to further promote your brand. The tool is not free. As such, you need to determine whether it's what your business needs considering the budget you are running on.

Quintly

Observing how your brand is performing against your rivals in the same industry is key to knowing whether you are doing well or not. With Quintly tool, you will get insights on how your brand is fairing as compared to your rival brands. If the performance is way below your expectations, then you need to make necessary adjustments. Far from this, the tool will also help you in getting the right influencers for your marketing campaign.

Followerwonk

If your business will be using Twitter mostly to market its brand, then Followerwonk is the tool to have. The tool aids in ranking your followers based on the number of people that are following them. This means that you can track your audience as a way of increasing your brand's visibility.

Mention

Just as the name suggests, the tool will help you in tracking mentions of specific keywords on social media. This is a common tool that is used by businesses marketing their brands on social media. It tracks down hashtags, product names, brand names, etc. You only need to specify the keywords that you need to be tracked.

The mentioned tools are just but a few of the many tools that are using in making social media marketing effective. It is important to note that your choice depends on your business marketing goals. So, it is highly recommended that you carefully compare and settle for those that suit your business needs. If you are running on a tight budget, you might want to opt for tools that are free to use. Nonetheless, don't be too stingy as successful marketing demands that you invest in marketing.

MeetEdgar

MeetEdgar is another reliable social media tool that gives you the ability to recycle some of your old posts. While using this tool, you only need to arrange your posts based on content. The tool with then schedule the posts depending on the categories you made.

Tagboard

As you plan to listen to your audience effectively, Tagboard is a handy tool for the job. It makes your work easier by scanning through your follower's comments. For instance, if you wish to know the discussions around a particular hashtag, you simply need to specify it. Tagboard will then scan all comments made on that hashtag. From this, you get to find out more about brand mentions. Equally, it will help you in understanding your customers better. The posts that have numerous comments will imply that this is what your customers love to talk about. Therefore, you can then go ahead and personalize your posts to meet their expectations.

Bitly

There are those URLs that you would want to shorten so that they can fit appropriately on your social pages. Bitly does just that. It helps you in shortening your URLs in a desirable way. Once the URLs have been posted to different social media pages, you can then use the tool to gain insights on how the links are performing.

Tweepi

Tweepi will help you in getting more followers. The tool is easy to use. It gathers your information about Twitter users that would be interested in what you offer. Thereafter, it also gives you an easier way by helping you engage with them through mentions. Alternatively, you can follow them. Therefore, this tool is handy if you wish to increase your user engagement more so if your followers are mostly active on Twitter.

Brand24

Brand24 will help you in finding out what people are saying about your product or company in general. With the help of this tool, you will not miss out on any mentions about your brand. The best part is that you can get insights of brand mentions from other social media pages. Through this information, you can then segment your audience and focus on those that have a high influence on your brand.

Agorapulse

Another ideal tool that you might come across in the market is Agorapulse. This tool brings together all your social media accounts in a single dashboard. Hence, you don't need to hover around checking comments from all your social media pages. Monitoring your social media activity is therefore made easy. You also get the benefit of scheduling posts with the features that are at your disposal.

The tools discussed in this section should not limit you from using what you think is fit for your business. Keep in mind that some of these tools are not free. Thus, you will need to dig in deeper into your pockets to use them. Before settling for any tool, confirm that it is a tool that has a proven track record. Do some research to find out whether other businesses are also using it. Certainly, a good tool will have positive references all over. Make a wise choice that will make your social media marketing experience exciting. Perhaps the best thing that you can do is to find out which tools your competitors are using. Thereafter, take your time to decide whether the tools will also suit your business.

Final Thoughts

Taking everything into account, social media marketing is crucial for the success of your business. You are not marketing on social media just because other businesses are doing it. You are selling on social networks as this is what your business needs. The statistics tell it all; over 2 billion people are using social media to communicate. These are the people that depend on your products and services. The advantage of using social media is that they have been brought together to form of a community. Therefore, your business could easily reach them with the promotional messages that they have.

From what has been said, social media marketing is not an easy task. It is also not difficult. However, there are secrets to making the best out of your social media campaign. Companies are making millions from the ads that they post on their social networks. Interestingly, there is nothing unique about them. What differentiates them from what you are doing is the strategy you utilize. A different strategy will determine the success or failure of your promotion. If you fail to have a plan, then you are certainly planning to fail.

There are several social media platforms that you should turn to. To name a few, Facebook, YouTube, Instagram, and Twitter are among the best platforms that businesses exploit. Knowing the right platform that you should focus on is important. This begins with first understanding who your audience is. For example, if most of your followers are from Facebook, then your marketing efforts should focus more on posting on Facebook.

However, it doesn't mean that you should disregard other social networks that your business has profiles. Finding the right balance in using all your social media pages is important. Remember, the main aim of your marketing campaign is to boost your reach and engagement. Therefore, you need to have a diverse social media presence. Your company should be well represented on Facebook, Twitter, and the likes.

What you post on your social pages matters a lot. What kind of messages are you sending to your audience? Will these messages portray your brand in a good way? Will they sell you in the best way possible? Content is key to winning over a huge following. As such, it is wise to research your clients and understand the content that motivates them greatly.

Perhaps you might have thought that the entire social media marketing process is a nightmare. Well, sorry to say this but, it is indeed a challenge. However, have you thought about the numerous tools that you can utilize? There are various management tools that you can use to boost your brand's growth quickly. For instance, Hootsuite tool will bring together all your social media pages in one dashboard. Accordingly, you will find it easy to post content and monitor performance all in one page. The social media analytics tools will come handy each time you need convenience. So, don't forget to make good use of the tools discussed herein.

The same tools will also help you in tracking your performance. How good is your content performing? How are your audiences responding to your posts? What kind of posts are doing well? These are some of the questions that the data analytics tools will help you answer. Eventually, you will be a successful marketer as you get to improve with time.

Before you begin the marketing process, sit down and draft a plan. Find a plan that works for your business. The strategy should give you a roadmap on how you will handle the entire marketing campaign. Without this plan, you will find it challenging to overcome several challenges that will come your way. What you need to know is that challenges are there to make you stronger. The best way of dealing with them is by being prepared to face them. This is part of your overall social media marketing strategy.

Ask yourself why you are marketing your brand on social media. There are tons of conventional marketing strategies that you could have opted to use. Nevertheless, you decided to use social media. Why? Is it because other businesses are doing it? Is it because your target market mostly uses social media? Or is it because you want to build your brand? Well, we all have varying reasons as to why you need to invest in social media as a marketing tool. The most important thing is to make the right decision that will have a positive impact on our businesses.

Marketing on social media is the right thing to do. Convincing reasons as to why you should do this has been mentioned in this book. Think about the fact that marketing on social media is cost-effective. Thousands of companies are using social media to market their brands because it is free. This implies that they end up getting better returns on their investments as compared to conventional forms of marketing. There is paid advertising that you could also turn to on social media. Nevertheless, it is vital that you first determine the plan that suits you before rushing to settle for anything.

Besides the aspect of cost, social media is also a great place to increase your brand visibility. Just as you use social media for personal reasons, you can also use it to boost your business' visibility. With the significant number of people accessing the internet every day, you can be sure that you will have a large following on social media. Keep in mind that a lot will be required from your end including your creativity. Standing out from thousands of other businesses offering similar products is not easy. Hence, you need to bring out your big guns for this occasion.

So, the ball is in your court; this book has given you the secrets that you need to become a successful marketer on social media. Stick to the recommendations that have been noted and rest assured that your rivals will keep track of your social media activity. As you market your brand on social media, always remember that the platform gives you a similar marketing advantage just as the big players in the market have. Therefore, you need to work on converting your followers into loyal customers. Don't just take pride of the thousands of followers that are on your page. Make a point of utilizing the effective strategies of converting your followers. No magic is used here. The discussed plans are some of the things that you might have been aware of. You only need to do things in a manner that is in line with what your audience needs.

Make a wise move today that will have a positive impact on your business tomorrow. Begin by investing in the best social media pages that have been discussed in this material. Next, work your way up to utilize other social platforms that have not been mentioned. With time, you will garner a deeper understanding of the best platforms that suit your business. Your audience will determine the pages that will work for you. Therefore, don't sweat over this. Just rely on social media analytics tools to ensure that you make sound conclusions regarding how your brand is fairing out there.

Gary Jake

If you find this book helpful in anyway a review to support my endeavors is much appreciated.

www.ingramcontent.com/pod-product-compliance
Lightning Source LLC
Chambersburg PA
CBHW071548210326
41597CB00019B/3163